Above all else, guard your heart, for everything you do flows from it.

Proverbs 4:23

Latayne dedicates this
to her precious grandchildren.

Beth dedicates this to the kids
who continue to teach her:
Lana, Gerrit, and Dawson.
They inspire and motivate her.

Contents

ONE

Get Real

Last semester, I walked away from the psychology class I teach to university freshmen and had to stand for a moment to absorb what *they* had taught *me*. I was floored.

"What do parents need to know about teens and sex?" I had asked them.

The cumulative answer was, "Everything. They are clueless."

Waitaminute. We've had sex, that's how we produced kids. We know all about hormones because we remember their house-on-fire effect on us.

We're hip. We know all about #MeToo and workplace sexual harassment, with human resources rules we can practically recite by rote. We've got this.

Except we don't. According to kids today who are just coming out of their teens, we have no idea how sexually saturated their world is. And how nearly worthless many of us have been in helping them navigate it.

Why do they say we're clueless?

Parents are often "one and done" when it comes to personalized sex education for their kids. We have "the talk," or

send them to a seminar, or give them a book, and then dread/
hope they'll come to us with further questions. But they usually don't. They want casual, everyday conversations about it.
If it's going to get awkward, a Wikipedia article won't judge
them for asking.

Today's boundaries confuse kids. They understand that people
get in trouble and can lose their jobs or celebrity status because of
#MeToo issues, but some young males are understandably anx-
ious and confused about what the lines are that they can't cross,
what could get them arrested. And girls watch videos and think
being sexy/powerful has nothing to do with being victimized.

- That whole no-dating and purity pledge thing confused
  us too. True, it provided some overt boundaries, but even
  its pioneers now admit that by guaranteeing great sex for
  those who wait until marriage, the realities of newlywed
  life crushed many who never developed a healthy view
  of the synergy between sexuality and spirituality. (What?
  You didn't know there's a synergy? Read on!)
- In past years, talking to teens about sex assumed binary
  genders—male and female. Now homosexuality and a
  spectrum of behaviors up to and including omnisexual-
  ity (sexual attraction to people of all genders and ori-
  entations) have muddied the waters for teens, and even
  more for their parents.
- Kids aren't aware that you may actually know about
  all these things, so they assume you don't. Because you
  don't talk about it to them.

A Reality Check

Teenagers today were born immersed in technology, and they're
oblivious to how it subsumes their lives. You won't be surprised

to learn that fully 95 percent of teens have access to a smart-phone, 45 percent say they are online "almost constantly," and 90 percent say they play video games.[1]

What has this virtual reality taught them?

- Entertainment and social media depict casual, uncommitted sex as normal between unmarried people. For youth, it's a landmark of growing up, similar to getting a driver's license. (We as parents tell them how to avoid wrecks and not to drink and drive; we also tell them how to protect themselves against pregnancy and disease—thereby implying that teens' active sexual behavior is as much a given as driving.)

- Almost everything in their world says that homosexual sex is good to explore, and that authentic gender identity is what the individual (even a toddler) says it is.

- There's no sense of the sacred in sex. Teens aren't awed by sex—if not "down and dirty," it's at least commonplace.

- Be prepared for variety—like when your boyfriend wants anal sex, as a *Teen Vogue* article described for young females.[2]

But Here's the Real Surprise

If teens don't know how to navigate the mysterious world of sexual practices, they are even more unsure about real, lasting relationships. Surprisingly, while parents are trying to figure out how to prevent their kids from having sex too early or with the wrong people, today's youth just fade into the less-risky fantasy world of technology.

Listen, parents! *They're not having more sex, they're having less.* One 2015 Centers for Disease Control study said that 60 percent of high school students had not had sex before they graduated from high school.³ As we will see in later chapters, many young people are scared to death about intimacy in any form. They are highly educated in sex, they just don't engage in sexual behaviors as much as teens did in the past.

I also asked college freshmen about Christian values and sexuality. While most might agree that homosexuality is wrong, they are very fuzzy about whether what's wrong are homosexual inclinations or just homosexual behaviors. I give them the scenario of two unmarried sexually active gays who want to come to their church, and the freshmen conclude that someone should teach the couple the appropriate Bible verses about homosexuality, and if they won't accept those teachings and make behavioral changes, then they obviously don't believe the Bible and shouldn't go to that church.

But then I give a similar scenario, except the couple is "straight," and one person is having an extramarital affair. The students reason that church leaders should give him or her Scriptures about adultery, but usually the students' responses indicating the couple should be cut off aren't as strong as with homosexual couples. With heterosexual couples, students are more likely to respond that church leaders would counsel the individuals and work with them to honor their commitments.

This helps students recognize that our response to sexual situations often isn't just biblical; it's also informed by our own family culture and beliefs. We can't blame them. Most of us aren't even sure about what we think are reliable boundaries and definitions. Test yourself with these scenarios.

You drop by your son's new apartment at college to bring him groceries, and his roommate, who is wearing just underwear, answers the door. On the couch, you see a partially clothed young man. They say your son will return later, so after introducing yourself, you leave the groceries.

- What would you expect your son to do?
- What if your son assured you the couple were in a monogamous, committed relationship?
- Would it change your assessment if your son's roommate were female?
- Would it have been different if it was your daughter's apartment?
- What if you had found this situation at your own house after coming home unexpectedly?
- What if your son or daughter was thirteen? Or sixteen?

One of your son's friends lingers after a church party at your house. "I need to talk to you," he tells you. "I know this will sound weird, but I feel like I'm a girl trapped in a boy's body. I don't know what to do or who to talk to."

- What would you tell this teen?
- Would this disclosure change your feelings toward him? Toward your son's friendship with him?
- What would you say to help?

Relatives are coming for a visit, and you've asked your son to clean up his room so your sister and her husband can sleep there. You are disappointed at the still-messy room, and as you straighten your son's desk, you hit the mouse and the monitor flickers on and displays a pornographic picture.

- What would you expect your son to do?
- How would this change your interactions with your son?
- Would you react differently if it were your daughter's room?

Ah. Not so easy. What made you uncomfortable? What was downright intolerable? But more important, will your discomfort be a barrier to discussing these totally possible situations with your teen?

Test Yourself

Christians shouldn't have to operate on feelings or "situation ethics" if we have some clear biblical guidelines, right? However, our parents may not have covered that with us in "the talk." Most of our instructions about sex from our own parents may have been, in essence, "Don't do it till you're married." And "it" is never described or discussed.

Test yourself here to see if you know what the Bible actually says about some of these issues. Grab a Bible, a pencil, and a concordance to answer these questions. You may have to ask a pastor for help.

1. What does the Bible teach about sex in the context of a marriage relationship?
2. What guidelines does the Bible provide for helping teens set physical and sexual boundaries when they are dating?
3. What does the Bible teach about masturbation?
4. What does the Bible teach about abortion?
5. What does the Bible teach about sex outside of marriage?
6. What does the Bible teach about homosexuality?
7. What does the Bible teach about rape and incest?
8. What does the Bible teach about pornography?
9. What does the Bible teach about gender fluidity?

What your kid will naturally want to know even if they don't ask: Once you've figured out what the Bible says about these issues, are you involved with any of these practices? And what are you doing about it? We will discuss how to address these issues later in the book.

What God Intended Sex to Be

The first question may be the most essential one, because in talking about sex with our kids, we often emphasize the negatives, the "what not to do." (True, there's "Do not handle! Do not taste! Do not touch!" in Colossians 2:21–23, but this Scripture shows that forbidding alone is of limited value.)

We don't know how to talk about the other side of the coin, the ideal of Christian sexuality, that it is a way to actually reflect something about humanity's relationship with God. It might make you uncomfortable to learn, for instance, that in the Old Testament, the Hebrew word for "know," as in knowing another individual, is the same word for *sexual relations*. So when Jeremiah says you can brag about knowing God,[4] he's not ignoring the implications of intimacy that are far above mere acquaintance.

We don't think to say out loud to our kids that Christian sexuality has two forms: expressed in marriage or expressed in celibacy. Sexual urges, created by God, don't just evaporate with time. We just kind of gloss over all those Scriptures that talk about healthy people with normal sexual urges who choose not to act on them—ever. Sometimes we have to teach ourselves to see such celibate people as heroic role models, as are faithful husbands and wives.

It may be a new thought to us that God created the identity of sexual beings when He created us male and female.[5] But that's at the core of everything teens need to know about sexuality. God himself, at the apex of His creativity, put an identifying mark on each of our bodies to indicate something important, both about *identity* and *function*.

Talking Points with Your Teen: The Logo

I want to help parents here, and in upcoming chapters, to have accessible talking points for discussions with their teens. Jesus used stories and visual imagery to get points across, and I want to do the same.

For instance, kids understand logos and brands on genuine products, whether athletic shoes or clothing or software. The logo is the sign that the designer—who created the footwear or clothing or game—put originality, effort, testing, and personal attention into the thing he or she designed.

The designer cared about details, those things that make the product unique and special. With human beings individually designed by God, the details are down to the cellular level. No matter what you look like or make yourself look like on the outside, inside every female are female cells. Inside every male is male DNA. It's the logo of God, who created male and female in His image, that each person is born male or female.[6]

Okay, our sexuality shows our identity, right down to the genes. What does each person's sexuality say about what they are to do with it (function)? Kids understand that you can use brand-new designer jeans to scrub muddy floors. Or you can take a new $2,000 pair of celebrity sneakers and use them for soup ladles. They probably would work. But why would you? They were designed to help someone stand out. Sneakers help you compete athletically. Clothes make a statement about what's important to the wearer.

Our bodies were designed for even more worthy things. In each person's sexuality, your body carries the logo of its Designer, His intentions for your identity and your functions. It is supposed to be a symbol of your priorities, your focus, your destiny. Even more than that, it is supposed to get the individual to think about the Designer.

Each person is one of a kind, unique, and autographed. And like designers do, God numbers what He has made ("And even the very hairs of your head are all numbered. So don't be afraid; you are worth more than many sparrows," Matthew 10:30–31). Like a master artist, He keeps a record of His people—engraved on the palms of His hands.[7]

These are issues your teen wants to know about. If they have questions, they're going to get information somewhere. Teens are right—this world is saturated with sexuality. But not the way you think it is.

EXPLORATION
FOR PARENTS

In upcoming chapters, I'll give you some conversation starters and other ways to interact around your teen's understanding of his or her sexual self. But now that you've read this chapter, these questions are for you.

1. What information in this chapter surprised you? Can you think of how you could share this with your teen by saying something like, "I never knew xyz. What do you think about that?"

2. What lessons did you learn about sexuality as a teen that still influence you today? What can you conclude you should learn from that?

3. Since many teens are not participating in sexual behavior, they need a biblical view of celibacy. Read the words of Jesus in Matthew 19:11–12, where He said not everyone could live with the difficult requirements of marriage. How many of your interactions with your

children have expressed the possibility that God may want them to be celibate their whole lives, not just during their teenage years? Or do you think marriage is an ideal, and singleness a lesser state?

4. Television and movie depictions of parents often show them as people who obstruct the healthy and natural sexual exploration of teens. Contrast this with Proverbs chapters 4 and 5. Look in these two chapters for details about how a parent's interactions and instructions protect a teen's sexual self. Write yourself some notes.

5. If you were making a pie chart of your leadership of your children in sexual matters, what percentage is love and empathy as you remember your own feelings of teenage angst? What percentage is instruction? How much instruction comes from the Bible or a pastor? What percentage is seeking outside help? Are you satisfied with those percentages? If not, what strategies can you use to change the proportions?

6. Disney movies and much of popular culture teach children that they have the solutions to their own problems within themselves if they just look hard enough. If you are willing to agree that God created an orderly world, what does it mean to you that you were born before your children? In other words, do you see any implications in the idea that God's chronology allowed you at least a couple of decades to prepare to reason biblically with your children?

TWO

God's Plan for Sex

Jesus, the master storyteller, modeled the way to make memorable points with vivid stories. Following His lead, each topical chapter after this one will contain a real-life scenario from my experience and counseling practice, to tell you about real people with real situations and how they navigated the white-knuckle, white-water rapids of teens and their sexual issues. Sexuality isn't a single issue, it's a suite of issues. With each one, I'll share research, practical advice, and seasoned experience.

But you could get that in a secular book on the subject, and you're reading this book because you want to know how to raise *godly* sexual souls in their bodies to adulthood.

I want to share in this chapter essential concepts I will expand on later, issues that perhaps you'll need to explore and review several times. I'm assuming you have and want Christian values and a Christian lifestyle, but finding a way to first make those part of your own heart-thinking can be difficult. Once you do, you'll have a foundation for how to talk to your kids about some challenging subjects.

Just as you probably won't digest all these concepts the first time you read them, consider that a lesson for you in how kids will take time to digest a lot of things you tell them. Just as you might need to reread at your leisure and even do further research, your child will need to hear concepts repeated, considered, and applied in casual conversations that will let them know you're open to talking about sexual subjects.

Foundational Issue #1: It's Supernatural

Our culture is drenched in the supernatural. Take a look at movie and television listings and see how many of them deal with fantasy. You might rightly say that your teen knows the difference between superhero movies and reality, but this belief in the supernatural tries to fill a God-shaped hole in people's souls. People want to be entertained, but they also want to believe in a power they can't see, and right now they are believing in astrology, tarot cards, and crystals, among other things.[1]

Don't let your familiarity with Christianity make you forget that it is by definition a supernatural religion with a superhero Savior. On a certain calendar date two thousand years ago, a man who had been dead for three days got up and walked around. People went to violent deaths voluntarily because they staked their lives on this supernatural historical event. And the apostle Paul said that if you don't believe in that supernaturalness, there's no great eternity for you. Period.[2]

What's the takeaway for you and your teen? You have to decide if *you* believe this. And if you do believe that God has that kind of power over even death, then you're going to have to talk to your teen about it. And about the record of that kind of God in the Bible as being more true than their own memories or personal journals because their memories and journals are impacted by their personal views and biases. The Bible is even "more true" because it does not change and is not influenced by our experiences and perspectives.

Don't leave this up to your church and take your chances that your kid will gain faith by osmosis. There are many books and online resources available that will help you kick-start conversations about our supernatural God; some of my recommendations appear at the end of this book.

With this enormous responsibility comes an equally enormous blessing. That supernatural God is the ultimate Parent, who promises to help you in all the crazy parts of your life. He knows all about parenting. *And He invented sex.* Whoa. The Inventor gives you not only the owner's manual for the human body, but also promises to supernaturally help you. What you can do:

- Make a list of some "talk to your kid about God" resources if that's a lack you're feeling. Ask other parents. Beg, borrow, or buy one and read it.[3]
- Ask your pastor to help you with resources if you don't know how to affirm to your child (or yourself) that the Bible is historically true and reliable.
- Research shows that kids *want* to trust their parents, and actually crave interaction with them on important issues. And remember that if you're going to talk to them about penises and vaginas, you should be able to talk about God without stuttering.

Foundational Issue #2: What It Means to Be a Human

This used to be a topic for dusty old philosophy classes, but I guarantee that your teen is swamped with conflicting messages about what a human is.

On the one hand, without God, humans are depicted by the world as the end product of an evolutionary process, who formed groups that made up the rules about humanness as they went along. Since we are now so "advanced," teens are being told anyone can make such decisions individually. Specifically, anything that is on or in (as in the case of a pregnancy) one's body is that individual's property. So teens are led to believe that the authentic "self" is the mind, and the body is a morally inert substance, with strength and hormones and appearance that can be used—or adapted—at will. (No wonder our culture has such a fascination with zombies—the very picture of an active body separated from its mind and soul.)

Foundational Issue #3: God Invented Sex

Just as a person is a knitted-together body and spirit,[4] sex is all about identity and purpose too. A person is a combination of a specific body plus its spirit, united in identity and purpose. Similarly, true sex is between a specific man and a specific woman in a way that knits *them* together. Even visually, the human body shows that a penis fits into a vagina in a way that no other combination of appendages and orifices does. And all of this, likewise, has purpose.

One purpose is for reproduction. The human race can't continue without reproduction. Despite technology's advances,[5] for a unique individual to be created, it takes a sperm from a male (with male cells from birth) to be united to an egg from a biologically identified cell-deep woman.[6] (You can see from this cumbersome definition of *reproduction* that even simple terms like *man* and *woman* have become difficult to convey.)[7]

A second purpose of sex is for pleasure. Kids probably get this without too much explanation. What they may not get, unless you tell them so, is that sexual pleasure can be terrific because God planned it that way. God planned for sex to be terrific in a marriage relationship where two people know each other intimately and exclusively. It's the *opposite* of rebellion against God's plan to thoroughly enjoy sex. However, even that pleasure has both identity and purpose.

Let's identify *purpose* first. Sex is anything but one and done. It makes you want to keep coming back for more. God knew that—He designed it. One of its primary features is that it is satisfying and so irresistible that it binds people together, to keep them coming back to each other for more. This is intended between one man and one woman for life, because on a level we will never fully understand, it knits one man and one woman together; the Bible says they become "one flesh."[8] This is not restrictive, it's solidifying. It's bedrock.

You can't fully understand this because it is a divine design. Your teen surely won't. But he or she needs to hear you say it. Over and over. One man and one woman, for life.

Even more than that, sex conveys *identity* in a way no other thing on earth can. No, we're not talking about altering your body to make it kind of match something called identity in your head. Sex, the knitting together of male and female, is perhaps the most effective 2,000-year-old ad campaign of Christianity to the world. Why do I say that?

Male-female lifelong commitment of body and spirit is a flashing billboard of how God runs the universe. The invisible God, as unseen but as undeniable as each of our own personal spirits, came to earth in a body. (See, the invisible combined with the visible.)

But Jesus, God in a body, after living here, left the earth with an enhanced version of that body. He demonstrated that although bodies look temporary in the messiness of death, through resurrection they are eternal just like the soul.

But what He didn't leave behind was His commitment to earth's inhabitants. Jesus, who never married, decided to treat the group of believers throughout history as His wife. Ephesians chapter 5 talks about the husband-wife relationship (one of mutual respect, mutual submission, mutual self-sacrifice) and caps off the discussion with this blockbuster:

> "For this reason a man will leave his father and mother and be united to his wife, and the two will become one flesh." This is a profound mystery—but I am talking about Christ and the church.[9]
>
> (vv. 31–32)

Wow! This is great stuff! It's multilayered and delightful and intriguing! It changes what we "know" about God.[10] Understanding this changes our view of marriage. It changes our view of sex. It elevates our minds to focus on God's purpose and to dedicate our lives to His work. Can you digest enough of that to believe it and to convey this to your teen?

Foundational Issue #4: Sin Has a Template

This is a short one, but it's really important. It will help both you and your teen if you can keep it in mind. *Sin has a template.*

The first sin in the Bible was committed, remember, by formerly ideal people with a perfect Parent. So it happens to everyone. And you can overlay the pattern of that first sin on every other sin in the Bible, in human history, in your life, and in your teen's life. The template has five elements. Read Genesis 3:1–7 to see how sin barrels through this template like a freight train.

1. God has rules. (Actually, not a lot of them, because they're broad enough to cover everything.) I'd paraphrase His first rule to Adam and Eve like this: "I gave you the entire world, and I ask you not to eat from one single tree. Take my word for it, it's a killer" (Genesis 2:16–17). For a teen, the restriction on sex (one man,

one woman, for life) is an example of a similarly simple rule.

2. A person (or a situation) will just show up that will ask you to reinterpret those rules: "Did God really say . . . ?" For teens this may happen in the classroom or in the back seat of a car, where they begin racking their brain for specific reasons why they shouldn't be there.

3. Once you start wondering, you may recite back the rules, even add to them, but you listen to the other point of view. (Teens are taught to respect others' points of view.) And by considering them, they can enter mentally into another world, one in which there's no such thing as sin if two people like what they're doing.

4. What you previously thought was wrong, you'll conclude, could be very right. Not only that, you will decide God can't do anything about it except try to restrict your freedom, and you're smarter than that. Teens fear ridicule. They fear that their parents' restriction of them is motivated by the old folks' utter ignorance of how the world really is. And God? Older. More irrelevant.

5. You will really, really want to use your own judgment plus what your body wants plus what you imagine the benefits will be. In fact, that's kind of godlike. You are making your sexual pleasure the god of your life rather than following your Creator. And there's no feeling in the world as powerful and exhilarating as sex.

And then—*and then!* The hammer of consequences falls. And especially with sexual sin, you can pay for the rest of your life. There are consequences of sin. You've seen it, haven't you? Usually the longer a sexual sin goes on, the bigger the cleanup.

Final Words

Now, this talking with teens will get messy. Keep in mind, if you can recall, how you felt about sex when you were a teen. It was the great unknown. It was mysterious and painful and confusing. And, if you are like most people, you've had experiences that were so primeval and gut-wrenching and exhilarating that you were pretty sure you were the only person who had felt sexual urges that intensely in the entire history of the world.

And then there's the issue of honesty about your own sexual experiences. You may have to hold on by your fingernails to the fact that God forgives your own sins and throws them into the depth of the ocean.[11] But such experiences aren't wasted—far from it. You can use them for empathy for your kids, and the bitterness of regret as a stir stick in your soul.

Should you confess to your kids all you did wrong sexually if they ask you? Think carefully about this. It may be that others would be deeply hurt if you did so. Remember you are dealing with your children, not a peer. Don't put your teen in the position of having to support you emotionally. You need to process your own regrets with an adult, not your child.

Keep in mind that you're the grown-up here. God also showed His purpose and design in human history in having you born first and then your kids. You can say, "I'm not ready to talk about that now, but maybe I can in the future." Or, "I understand just how hard it is to resist sexual urges, and someday we'll share how we were able to triumph in them." Or, "Thank God for His forgiveness, and I don't ever want to test Him on that again."

I can assure you, after decades of counseling teens, kids are very resilient. You will mess up when you talk to them. But it's better to make mistakes than to abandon your kid to this world. In the words of author John Maxwell, "Fail early, fail often, but always fail forward."[12]

You've got the totally supernatural Holy Spirit inside you. A body and soul Jesus bled out to pay for. And you've got the full weight of the great Designer God behind you. You can do this.

EXPLORATION
WITH YOUR TEEN

In the interaction section of this and the following topical chapters, I'll give you some conversation starters to use with your teen. If you don't know where to begin, you can always refer to a television show, movie, or event from your teen's life. Ask open-ended questions like "I was wondering what you thought about this?" or, "Have you ever heard of that before?"

Here are some other ideas.

1. Choose an example familiar to your teen in which a biblical character sinned. Discuss with your teen: What is the template for that sin? (Look back at our description of the template from Genesis 3:1–7.) How can we apply the template to this situation? Then choose a familiar nonbiblical story or an example from real life of a young person who went off track in their faith. Apply the template again to this situation.

2. Entire books have been written on our culture's deliberate separation of the concepts of body and mind, and the subject is too deep to cover here.[13] But the following are some ways to begin to explore this with your children (I'd take these in order):

   • Discussion Topic: Is it possible for the mind and the body to be separated? What do we call that condition? (Does the fact that this happens only at death tell you how essential each is to the other?)

- Discussion Topic: Read Genesis 2:7: "Then the LORD God formed a man from the dust of the ground and breathed into his nostrils the breath of life, and the man became a living being." Question: Was Adam a "person" when he was just dust? How do we know he couldn't similarly be just the breath of life?
- Discussion Topic: Read about when God created everything in Genesis chapter 1. How does each thing He created have a specific identity? How does everything He created have a specific purpose? How do we know He was utterly, completely satisfied with their identities and purposes?
- Discussion Topic: Read Psalm 139:13–14. What does the phrase "knit me together" imply about the body and the soul?
- Discussion Topic: Since God created human beings to be both body with spirit, knitted together in each individual womb, and created them specifically as "male and female," how does trying to change the overall gender appearance of your body show what could be considered profound disrespect for the individual bodies God created? Instead, what might be ways to treat our bodies with dignity, since they bear the image of God himself (Genesis 1:26–27)?
- Discussion: Do you own your body? Read 1 Corinthians 6:19–20 (emphasis added): "Do you not know that your bodies are temples of the Holy Spirit, who is in you, whom you have received from God? *You are not your own; you were bought at a price. Therefore honor God with your bodies.*" So if "ownership" can't describe your relationship with your body, what term might describe it better?

THREE

What's Happening Developmentally?

If you have a book or resource on adolescent culture and how it impacts development that is more than fifteen years old, throw it away. Adolescent culture has shifted dramatically and it is impacting development.

I've been a college professor for twenty-five years, and I can assure you that kids who come to me as freshmen today are far less emotionally mature, perhaps several years behind their counterparts of two decades ago. College freshmen are like high school freshmen were twenty years ago in almost every way that counts. The one exception is they mature physically faster than in past generations.

That means that if you were growing up in the eighties or nineties, you can't compare your teen to yourself at the same age. It just wouldn't be realistic.

Some of growing up is just the day-to-day negotiation of changes. Their bodies change. Their emotions can run wild. Whether or not they are accepted by their peers is crucial.

They're challenged intellectually at school. And you, as a parent, keep reminding them that their developing relationship with an unseen God has to trump all of those very solid factors.

These five areas of development—physical, emotional, social, intellectual, and moral/spiritual—are challenges for all kids. Teens don't necessarily deal with each of these issues at exactly the same time, but all teens deal with these developmental issues at some point in their adolescence.

Physical Development: What's Happening to Me?

Consider the case of one of my clients named Josh, who insists on wearing a jacket or hoodie in even the hottest weather. In any public setting he sits hunched down—on a couch, on the bus—anywhere except sitting up close to a table. At least one of his hands is always in his jacket pocket. Only after his parents bring him to me do I find out the problem. I assure him I've heard just about everything, and since he tells me he knows he's not getting out of this counseling room without explaining, he blurts it out.

"I get embarrassed," he starts. "I mean, I can't control things."

I nod and wait. He sighs and his face reddens.

"I get embarrassed. I get hard-ons and I can't do anything about it. I don't want everyone to see."

He's being ambushed by a body that just won't behave. He's all for this teenage thing and he likes his veins popping out on his arms and his voice deepening, but not this.

"This is normal for teen boys. All your friends have either already experienced it, are experiencing it, or will experience it," I tell him. "Eventually, your hormones will adjust and this won't happen nearly as often, but you are absolutely normal."

Josh and I go on to discuss strategies to help him conceal his embarrassment and adapt to his raging hormones.

Being a teen is confusing. Josh will also compare his developing body to those of his peers. The guys who develop more slowly are concerned that they're not masculine enough. Girls who develop earlier than their peers often don't have the emotional skill set to handle the sudden interest of guys who last year paid no attention to them. In fact, teens may interpret early or late development as being weird or disgusting.

The Changes of Puberty

Normally, the onset of puberty looks like this:

- Fat appears in female bodies and they develop breasts and their hips grow wider.
- Females begin menstruation, impacting their emotions and hormone levels on a monthly basis.
- Males begin experiencing voluntary and involuntary erections and ejaculations as their penis and testicles grow.
- Male voices deepen and begin to crack.

Females can start their periods as early as age eight and as late as sixteen. Because of this great variation in the timing of physical maturity, teens frequently feel very self-conscious. But the differences aren't imaginary and they have implications. For instance, females who physically mature faster than their peers are at a greater risk for depression, substance use, and early sexual behavior than their peers.[1] Males who mature early are more likely to have problems with peers later in adolescence and to experience depression,[2] and more likely to have their first sexual intercourse earlier than peers.[3] Late-maturing boys are more likely than other boys to be socially awkward, insecure, and variable in mood.[4]

The age of onset of puberty has been decreasing for decades. Currently boys are experiencing puberty at or just before age ten.[5] For girls, whereas the onset of menstruation was at the average age of sixteen or seventeen at the turn of the twentieth century, it is now twelve or thirteen.[6] No one knows why these earlier ages are the case, but some speculate that childhood obesity, dietary changes, and/or hormones in food may be factors.

Physical changes can be external as well as internal and not visible. It begins with the release of hormones in the brain; there are different levels of hormones in males and females, and infinite variations in the individuals of both sexes.

Both males and females have growth spurts and gain height and weight. Bones get longer and stronger, so teens can perform physical tasks they could not complete as children. The flip side is that they also develop body odor and acne, and they grow hair in new places.

Much of the physical change in puberty is embarrassing and often inexplicable. I remember an attractive teen girl named Emily who came to me, asking for a private conversation, and described that she was feeling sick to her stomach. My first thought was that she was pregnant, but as she continued talking, I eventually realized it was a different issue.

"It's just when I'm with Tyler," she says, describing a fledgling dating relationship of just a few weeks. Not pregnancy, I think. What, then?

She continues, describing flutters in her stomach and the sick feeling when he kisses her.

"I know it's weird. Nobody else gets sick when they kiss guys," she says. "What's wrong with me?"

There is nothing wrong with this teen, she just doesn't understand what is happening in her body when she is sexually aroused. She is interpreting sexual arousal as nausea because she doesn't have any previous sexual experience. It's all a funny feeling "down there."

As teens develop sexually, everything is a new experience: first wet dream, first kiss, first party, first love. The novelty of all these experiences contributes to the intensity of teen responses because they can't compare their current feelings and experiences with any other experiences. They wake up with pubic hair or pimples, their peer groups are a kaleidoscope, they don't know what's next in algebra, and parents keep changing the rules. Each of these areas of change creates anxiety for the teen because they are first-time experiences that can be just as disorienting as learning to drive. Eventually, their bodies quit changing and they become more comfortable with who they are, but most don't come equipped with the necessary skills for handling puberty alone.

We can look back at our own development, and in hindsight it seems pretty methodical. For a teen, it can be an unsettling, open-ended experience. They can't imagine themselves fully matured, or at ease in social situations, or writing a senior essay, or being able to share the Gospel with an unbeliever.

For many kids like Josh and Emily, puberty makes their bodies seem like they have suddenly become disconnected from them. Girls may panic at weight gain or losing their thigh gap and may begin seeing their bodies as enemies that have to be starved. Boys, when all their childhood dreams come true and they're finally bigger and more powerful than others, can see their bodies as tools that need to be bulked up and made even more formidable.

Keep reminding yourself that the Bible teaches that a human being is a body plus a soul. You will need to remind your teens that they are a knitted-together package of those two elements, and that they're not at war with each other even when it feels like their bodies are turning against them. One way of dealing with this is to discuss the difference between somewhat involuntary reactions—such as Josh's erection or Emily's physical response to her boyfriend—and following through on fantasies and ideations that follow such experiences. Your son or daughter needs to know that they will be fighting sexual temptation their whole lives, but just because you wake up from a wet dream doesn't mean you need to keep feeding a fantasy associated with it.

Since we know that Jesus started out as a baby and ended up as a grown-up, it might be helpful to remember that He, too, went through these developmental changes in His body. After all, He grew in both wisdom and stature—and that pretty much sums up physical and cognitive growth, right?

We don't know much about the adolescence of Jesus. The only story we have of that period of His life was about His getting lost, His parents' frantic search for Him, and the fact that His cognitive abilities were advanced.[7] But we can say with assurance that Jesus' body was unique because every single person God creates is unique. There were probably kids in His neighborhood who were taller or had facial hair before He did. He didn't match up to all His peers, and neither will your teen!

Galatians 6:3–5 is helpful and a good passage to discuss with your teen: "If anyone thinks they are something when they are not, they deceive themselves. Each one should test their own actions. Then they can take pride in themselves alone, without comparing themselves to someone else, for each one should carry their own load."

For teens who might start thinking their bodies are rebelling against them, they might see maintaining that unpredictable body as a "load." Parents can teach their children to take good care of their bodies by modeling the importance of eating healthy food and getting enough sleep. To encourage good nutrition, you can keep healthy snacks at home and limit junk food. Teens need sleep to grow, strengthen their bodies, and perform better academically. Strategize about how to put lights out and put electronic devices in "time out" at night. Even God rested!

I've often heard people say that if they'd known they were going to be in their bodies as long as they have been, they'd have taken better care of themselves earlier. You may not get much appreciation from your teen for watching out for their health right now, so do it for the sake of their future. One way you can express it to a teen is to tell them they are driving around in a luxury car like a Lamborghini right now, but they'll never be able to trade it in no matter how long they own it—so maybe they should take care of it.

A Note on Masturbation

Masturbation is stimulating one's own genitals for pleasure and self-comfort. The Bible does not directly address masturbation, but that's not because it is a new issue.

Many toddlers and preschoolers masturbate occasionally, and that's normal. Some discover that this is pleasurable while they are exploring their bodies. For others, it's consolation for an unhappy event such as having something taken away or after punishment. Once a child begins to masturbate, they rarely stop completely, but by age five or six they will begin to understand that it should be done only in private. Trying to completely forbid masturbation can send a message to our children that sex is a terrible thing, and may even lead to children feeling that their bodies are nasty. Rather than completely forbidding masturbation, a more effective approach would be to discuss God's intention for sexual relationships and how our bodies can experience pleasure, but that it is a private activity. As children get older, we need to discuss how engaging in masturbation may interfere with developing healthy sexual relationships with spouses once they are married. Completely forbidding children to engage in a pleasurable activity that they have discovered themselves may actually increase the likelihood that they will engage in the behavior. Once puberty arrives, masturbation usually increases again,[8] and it's more common among males of all age groups (73.8 percent reported it) than females (48.1 percent).[9]

Some people say the story of Onan in Genesis 38:3–10 is about masturbation (in fact, self-gratification and masturbation are sometimes referred to as "onanism"), but a close look at Onan's story shows it to be about a man who pulls his penis out during sexual intercourse (coitus interruptus) and ejaculates on the ground so as not to impregnate the widow of his brother.[10]

However, the Bible does warn husbands not to withhold themselves from their wives sexually (and vice versa) in 1 Corinthians 7:3–5. Men who masturbate rather than have sex with their wives certainly would fit in this category.

But how to talk to a teen about it? First Thessalonians 4:3–5 does say, "It is God's will that you should be sanctified: that you should avoid sexual immorality; that each of you should learn to control your own body in a way that is holy and honorable, not in passionate lust like the pagans, who do not know God." Someone who gets caught up in excessive masturbation will not describe it as "holy and honorable" as they let their body take control—sometimes to such an extent that they can scarcely think of anything else.

Think about it: Whenever a practice or object or goal takes the place of God, it becomes our master. Two Scripture passages address how easy it is to become enslaved (1 Corinthians 6:12 and 2 Peter 2:19–20). The Corinthians passage makes the point that even something that is permissible can still become your master if you allow it to.

Second Corinthians 10:5 tells us to "take captive every thought." You and your teen will agree: Some thoughts won't come along peacefully but have to be handcuffed and dragged.

Cognitive Changes: That Won't Happen to Me

One of the great realities parents don't recognize is that most teens thrive on risk. They operate on what we call a "personal fable"—the belief that normal consequences don't apply to their actions.[11] Educational programs and parents' warnings about sexual activities are often ineffective because teens quite literally believe they are immune to consequences. Interestingly, they are also unaware that they have this belief system. Therefore, trying to teach them about the aftereffects of sexual activities can be an extremely frustrating experience for adults. Fortunately, teens' bulletproof thinking is most prevalent during early and middle adolescence, and they begin to outgrow that concept as they develop more self-control and learn to evaluate what behaviors are acceptable and mature.

But there's a good side to teens' sense of invincibility: Trying new things gives teens the experiences that will help them transition to being independent adults (as long as their risk-taking is not fatal). Don't get your hopes up too early, though: When teens do develop the capacity to assess risks like an adult, they still often won't make safe choices because the pull of their emotions and peer pressure seem too great to them. You can protect your teen from unhealthy sexual risks by providing boundaries and supervision as well as discussing how to make safe decisions.

Teens are influenced by whether they have to make decisions on the spur of the moment or whether they have time to think about decisions. Of course, time and contemplation lead to safer and healthier decisions. This is a teachable skill. Two things you can do: One is to try to "buy time" in situations and help your teen delay decisions if possible. The old advice to sleep on it is good counsel for teens and their parents. Things often have quite a different complexion in the morning light. While anxiety and frustration may push teens to make an immediate decision, you can help them learn to take a deep breath and wait.

Another strategy is discussing ahead of time, or even role-playing, situations in which peers or authority figures may push them to make immediate decisions. For instance, teens need to know how to handle an invitation from a friend to a party where there's alcohol, or an invitation from a teacher to view porn. While neither of these exact situations may occur, your teen needs to be prepared to make decisions like these.

One of the best ways you can support your teen is by providing an out. One easy out for your teen is intrusive supervision. As a parent, show up randomly when your child is involved in a social event or extracurricular activity. Be "that" parent who checks up on your teenager. In addition, set up a password or phrase that indicates your teen wants you to say no. For example, if your teen normally calls you "Mom" but uses "Momma" during a text message or phone call, that means you need to tell your teen to come home right now and that he can't go with his friends. A system like this lets your teen save face and stay safe.

Final Thoughts

Different sections of the brain develop at different rates, with full development occurring in the mid-twenties. Significantly, the back part of the brain forms before the front. The back of the brain manages rewards, while the front part manages impulse control. Teens place a higher value on short-term rewards; knowing that helps you recognize how important social acceptance and immediate gratification are for teens. Think and strategize: "How can I provide immediate rewards when they make good decisions?" When your teen comes to you for help with a situation, reward them by helping them without judgment and by providing a tangible reward, such as letting them engage with peers in a safe environment. The next time something comes up and you need to provide guidance and redirection, you will have earned some credit with your teen with a positive experience.

As our teens' brains change, they are able to absorb facts, ideas, and skills more efficiently. It's a wonder to watch, so enjoy it! They are able to think abstractly for the first time and use advanced reasoning. Teens can even think about thinking. However, cognitive development, like physical development, happens at a different rate for everyone, so adolescents of the same age won't have the same thinking and reasoning skills. Keep telling yourself that your teen's brain won't be fully developed until they are at least twenty-five years old.

This is confusing for teens and adults too. Just as a teen's onset of physical puberty may not match the chronological age of their peers', a teen's thinking abilities may not match their appearance. They may look like they are in their right minds but be as shortsighted as a preschooler in a dollar store with a pocketful of quarters.

EXPLORATION
WITH YOUR TEEN

1. Luke 2:52 addresses adolescent development: "And Jesus grew in wisdom and stature, and in favor with God and man." In looking back over your own adolescent years, can you identify any specific persons, incidents, or conversations that helped you develop wisdom? Would any of them be what you would consider a turning point? Did they involve mistakes you made, or did you take advice gladly?

2. Looking at the Scripture above, how could the knowledge that Jesus went through puberty be helpful to your teen? Perhaps they've never considered that He went through some of the same developmental changes. How could you introduce that thought to them?

3. First Corinthians 13:11 has this statement from the apostle Paul: "When I was a child, I talked like a child,

I thought like a child, I reasoned like a child. When I became a man, I put the ways of childhood behind me." Discuss—and give credit to your teen for—the ways they think they have begun putting away childhood. Some of their answers may surprise you and lead to enlightening discussions.

4. How can Colossians 3:23–24, with its instructions to do tasks as if doing them for God, help your teen look at short-term goals (since they may not be able to process long-term goals at this point)? Here are some other Scriptures about short-term goals that are easy to put on sticky notes and/or memorize.

- "And if you do good to those who are good to you, what credit is that to you? Even sinners do that" (Luke 6:33).

- "And without faith it is impossible to please God, because anyone who comes to him must believe that he exists and that he rewards those who earnestly seek him" (Hebrews 11:6).

- "Ask and it will be given to you; seek and you will find; knock and the door will be opened to you" (Matthew 7:7).

- "Give, and it will be given to you. A good measure, pressed down, shaken together and running over, will be poured into your lap. For with the measure you use, it will be measured to you" (Luke 6:38).

- "God 'will repay each person according to what they have done'" (Romans 2:6).

- "Seek the LORD your God, you will find him if you seek him with all your heart and with all your soul" (Deuteronomy 4:29).

- "Humble yourselves before the Lord, and he will lift you up" (James 4:10).

FOUR

How Teens Relate to Others

In our previous chapter about teens' physical and cognitive development, something may have escaped your attention. It's the fact that while kids' bodies are maturing more quickly, other intangible aspects that combine with physicality to make them human—such as their decision-making, emotional, and social skills—seem to be lagging behind those of previous generations. If we return to the image of a luxury Lamborghini sports car for their teen bodies, many of these suddenly supercharged vehicles are being driven by emotions and thinking processes of grade-schoolers.

Imaginary Audience

One aspect of those thinking processes is egocentricity. Teens are often obsessed with their physical appearance. The term *imaginary audience* has been used to describe the way teens believe that everyone is watching them all the time.[1] Teens often believe that others are paying great attention to their appearance and thus may spend an excessive amount of time on it.

I remember when the parents of Meagan called me and described how their daughter gets up three hours before school to get dressed, spending over an hour on her hair alone.

"And if she gets a pimple, she won't go at all!" Meagan's mom said.

Meagan attends church and school and does her homework, but all her free time is spent "window shopping" online or looking at fashion magazines. This teen-typical egocentricity has Meagan convinced that everyone critiques her as she does herself. She feels a tremendous pressure to look "perfect."

Teens often define perfection as the athletes or models depicted in the media, all of whom create an unrealistic expectation and an unattainable standard for appearance. Meagan examines the airbrushed images and doesn't recognize that even the models themselves aren't capable of looking like that final product: Photo shoots are photoshopped. Anxiety about her appearance leads to anxiety with others—everybody must be scrutinizing her. It's not that Meagan is out of touch with her own feelings, but she relies more heavily on what she believes others might think.

Managing Emotions

Hormones in the brain that bring about physical changes also affect teens' emotional development. It's no news to you that teens have heightened emotional responses. During adolescence, teens experience things that are stressful for anyone, such as rapid changes in peer relationships, school expectations, and family dynamics. But when teens experience stress, they respond with more emotion than adults because their brains are not fully developed.

How can you help your teens learn to manage their emotions?

- First, help them recognize that the parts of the brain that develop last are those that help with problem solving and emotional regulation. Lower your expectations and accept that the Lamborghini can self-start and go from zero to sixty before the teen even realizes it is in gear.

- Emotions are strong and complex, sometimes beyond a teen's ability to talk about them. Teens can learn to express their feelings by
  - writing about them,
  - expressing their feelings through art,
  - listening to or performing music,
  - engaging in physical activity (one reason sports can be so important),
  - crying (give your teen—male or female—permission to cry), and
  - processing emotions with a trustworthy person.

Another way to help teens process emotions and thoughts about relationships and difficult issues is what's called the "empty chair technique."[2] If a teen is anxious about another person or a social situation, the teen imagines this person or situation in an empty chair. The teen sits in the chair and takes the role of the other person, saying what he or she imagines the other person would say. The teen then switches back to his or her own chair and says what he or she wants to say out loud to the other person. This exercise might feel awkward at first but can build sensitivity to another person's perspective and allow helpful expression of emotions.

Relaxation techniques can help calm teens' bodies and help them calm their anger or other strong emotions. Common relaxation techniques include

- deep breathing,
- slowly repeating a calming word or phrase while breathing deeply,

- visualizing a relaxing experience,
- participating in non-strenuous, slow exercise,[3] or
- wearing a silicone wristband or other jewelry as a reminder to wait a certain period before reacting.

Discuss with your teen that their emotional reaction may feel over the top but is not unmanageable. (All temptations, the Bible tells us, come with "a way of escape.")[4] Help them look for the way out with these normal strong emotions, examine the emotions, and help them see there can be negative consequences when they inappropriately express strong emotions.

Again, teens typically operate on the personal fable that consequences only happen to others, but the blowback from blowups can show them otherwise.

Heightened Empathy

There's good news and bad news about how physical changes increase teens' capacity for emotional awareness and empathy. They can be profoundly moved by identifying with someone or something else—for instance, witnessing a large number of people who become vegetarians in their teen years. But the bad news is that in our culture, most teens base their own worth on their enhanced sensitivity toward what people think of them, or how others view their personal successes.

You can put that empathy to work for a better cause, though, by harnessing your teen's heightened empathy and emotional response. Jesus told a story about the relative importance of physical matters versus spiritual ones, and about true worth. In Matthew 10:28–31, He said,

- *Do not be afraid* (He addressed that we will all get anxious.)

- *of those who kill the body* (Protecting and caring for your body is important but is not the most important thing.)
- *but cannot kill the soul.* (He knows there are dangers worse than physical ones.)
- *Rather, be afraid of the One who can destroy both soul and body in hell.* (This world is temporary, and even if we don't see consequences immediately, they will come.)
- *Are not two sparrows sold for a penny?* (God knows that kids and adults value things that others think are worthless.)
- *Yet not one of them will fall to the ground outside your Father's care.* (But God is always aware of their well-being, even more vigilant than security cameras in an airport.)
- *And even the very hairs of your head are all numbered.* (His hyper-concern about the tiniest parts of your body is so great that He numbers them.)
- *So don't be afraid;* (There's a reason not to be anxious.)
- *you are worth more than many sparrows.* (His care for your body and soul are exponential.)

Who Am I Today?

One Tuesday night a church youth group asked me to be an informal speaker. Valerie, whom I'd just seen with her family at a ball game the week before, was there. This night, it wasn't until someone called her name that I looked at her more closely. I hardly recognized her. She was dressed in a halter top and very tight jeans. I knew her parents would not approve of her attire.

As I greeted her, I reflected on the fact that she'd gone through several clothing styles in the last year or so. For a while her hair was forward in her face and she wore dark colors. A few weeks later she and her friends were wearing what I'd describe as vintage clothing I suspected had come from a thrift store.

This time was different. When she saw me, she rushed over and begged me not to tell her parents of this clothing style. So I immediately knew that Valerie understood her parents' values.

"I changed clothes at my friend's house before I came. Mom and Dad don't let me wear fun clothes," she explains.

While Valerie may not consciously decide who she wants to be *every* day, she is like many teens who try on new identities through changes in clothing, hairstyles, and jewelry. Identity exploration and formation is one of the most important developmental tasks of adolescence. Prior to adolescence, a child's identity is generally an extension of their parents'. Once they recognize they are not an extension of their parents' identities, teens begin to peel away from their parents and develop their own identities. This is natural and normal.

Their peers become their focus, and they begin to search for who they are and how they can fit in with them, trying to decide who they want to be or be like. They may announce who they are by wearing strikingly different clothing, like Valerie, or new hairstyles or cryptic jewelry that represent part of their identity.

They're not just exploring outward identity; they're also trying to integrate a new component of sexuality into their self-concept. This is a good thing: If a teen can clarify what they believe, they set a foundation for making healthy and responsible decisions about their own sexuality. However, teens may intentionally make choices that clash with their family's spiritual values as a way of distinguishing their own identity. A teen raised in a conservative religious home with parents who oppose abortion may participate in a pro-choice organization. Similarly, a teen whose parents have actively voiced the belief that schools should advocate abstinence rather than birth control may write an editorial for the school paper advocating the distribution of condoms. These "rebellions" are part of the developmental process of establishing a clear personal identity and are generally transient. However, as will be discussed in chapter 12 on gender issues, one of the responsibilities of parents is to allow their children to examine and discuss more major, permanent changes such as tattoos, while protecting them from making alterations to their bodies that cannot be reversed.

Parents have to meet their kids where they are. A firmer sense of identity makes them feel confident and competent. Questioning values and ideas, developing and looking for outlets for their talents such as musical ability or writing, and trying new activities are normal and good.

Value your teen's unique identity. God's logo and His autograph on their body and personality show how He delights in individuality. We are the great orchestra of His creativity, each playing a divinely made instrument. If we're all blaring out the same note continuously, where's the music? Where's the communication? He wants each person's unique sound to be heard: "Even in the case of lifeless things that make sounds, such as the pipe or harp, how will anyone know what tune is being played unless there is a distinction in the notes?" (1 Corinthians 14:7).[5]

God told the prophet Jeremiah that He formed him in the womb with a particular life mission in mind,[6] and it's reasonable to think that God has hopeful, great intentions for every one of His children and yours. And part of that greatness is that your teen is unique and shows the purpose of God in making a unique person.

Social Development

Your teen's social development may challenge your expectations and relationship with them. Whereas your younger children spend most of their time with their family, teens begin spending most of their time outside the family circle in school activities, sports, church groups, jobs, and other pursuits. If you think you are losing some control of your teen when this happens, it's true, and in the long run it's good. It's what your child needs to function with others. Peers and other mentors will begin to take over some of your roles as trusted allies. You're not being replaced, you're being replicated: Your many roles begin to be distributed.

Teens will typically have an increasing number of peers in their lives, and will begin incursions into those new circles, exploring people, social structures, and ideas. They take on leadership roles at church and school. In a very exciting way for them, cognitive and emotional development energize each other, and teens begin to have deeper conversations and express their emotions better. These interactions will teach them empathy and compassion, and how to evaluate new views.

Expanding circles of friends will inevitably expose your teens to additional sexual information and more opportunities to explore their sexual identity. While your children are developing a larger social circle and learning more about sexuality, they will need your support and guidance. They don't have the experience and life skills to recognize the kinds of dangers you can clearly see in relationships and situations that will harm them, whether with peers or authority figures. Stay in the game. Keep talking to them about sexuality and God's plan for sex in a way that shows you want them to expand their circles, to have the adventure of exploration, but in safe ways.

Environment impacts the rate of social development. Teens of the same age will have different abilities to handle social situations. For instance, teens who look more mature may be treated more like adults or interact more with older teens. Interactions with older teens may lead to more sexual situations and information. Teens do not own the emotional and social skills for these interactions: You're the one equipped and authorized to set safe boundaries and supervise their interactions as they learn new ways to make decisions and cope with challenging situations. On the other hand, teens who develop later may be treated more like children than teens. Such a teen will be frustrated about being treated like a child and will worry about when their sexual development will begin.

Younger teens tend to hang out with teens who are similar to them, while older adolescents tend to hang out with a greater diversity of peers. All will want to fit in somewhere, and the peer pressure can be positive as well as negative. Positive peer groups can help teens build relationship skills, develop a positive self-concept, and have confidence to take positive risks. But for the first time in history, a major factor of peer pressure isn't personal interactions but the very impersonal and sometimes devastating peer pressure of technology. We will discuss that in chapter 9.

Moral/Spiritual Development

The developing brains of teens help them assimilate morals and values that will grow and accompany them into adulthood. Their newfound ability to think abstractly allows them to think about the world more deeply. Whereas children see the world in black and white, teens begin to wrestle with the fact that not every question has a clear-cut answer. The shades of gray can help them have empathy for others as they consider their perspectives. But the development of empathy and the capacity to consider shades of gray can also be a dangerous combination as values about sexuality develop. Empathy for friends struggling with sexual issues can drive teens to question God's plan for sex: Does God not care how much their friends are hurting? If you as a parent keep the communication lines open so they see the value and reasonableness of Christianity, they can continue to factor that into their growing sense of right and wrong.

Children follow or rebel against rules. But teens go further and naturally question the reasons behind the rules. "Because I said so" becomes a call to battle. They want justifications for curfews, rules, and limits. Are they just? Are they for the good of the majority or a few? They aren't trying to be rude when they question the rules; they are developing their personal values and morals. They will ask these questions about sexuality as well, and rules and boundaries pertaining to sexuality will help teens develop their values. The debates about rules—you're the adult and you set the tone in debates—are the way teens begin to form their views of the world and how it should work. When teens get answers to their questions about rules, they are better able to see why a rule makes sense, and they are more likely to accept it. And you may learn that some of the rules you've followed without thinking should be examined. Be vulnerable. Think it out with them. Agree with them if something really is "just stupid."

For the first time, they are considering the big questions about what is right and wrong in the world. Social media, sexual imagery, pornography, homosexuality, and gender issues are all right in their face every day. They're startled to consider that moral dilemmas may not be just theoretical: They may have to make difficult choices about friends or ideas.

But don't forget that although they're considering these things, *their brains are still developing and they can't yet think like adults.* They're a work in progress, gaining the skills to adulting when they ask questions, challenge rules, and question people in authority. Through this process, teens refine their thinking about sexuality and emotional skills. Just as you'd encourage them when they are first batting a ball or learning to play the clarinet, they'll bobble it again and again. This powerful package of reasoning and emotional skills is a new instrument they're going to make some terrible music on, but they'll get it if you're patient and listen and let them make mistakes. And stick to your guns on the nonnegotiables, such as your faith in the power and the kind character of God. Let them know that faith has its reason, and many people depend on a personal conviction that their faith has supportive grounds.

Final Thoughts

As you acknowledge your teen's uniqueness and talents, keep in mind that they didn't get to choose their individual vulnerabilities. Think about yourself: Did you choose to be vulnerable to overeating or substances? To jealousy? To judgmentalism? To any disabling habit or sin you struggle with every day? Every human being has his or her own weaknesses, and we hate them. We hate, hate, hate them and would be rid of them if we could.

But you don't get to choose your weaknesses, and your teens don't get to choose theirs. The only choice is how you and they deal with those fixtures of their souls. The apostle Paul begged to have his own "thorn in my flesh" removed, and God's answer wasn't the removal but the addition of grace, supernatural strength to handle the weakness that never went away.[7] That's available to you, and to your teen too.

EXPLORATION
WITH YOUR TEEN

Exercise: Over a two- or three-week period, read with your teen aloud the Gospel of John. Find as many examples of Jesus' frustrations with life as you can. For instance, Jesus was the master communicator of all time but was often totally misunderstood. Teens also often feel they are communicating and not being heard. And parents certainly feel that way! After reading with your teen, make a chart or list of those frustrating situations in the life of Jesus. Post it on the refrigerator and talk about it.

Questions to discuss with your teen:

Can you name any situations in which Jesus was misunderstood or seemed to get frustrated? Which situations remind you of your own frustrations with not being understood? What can I as a parent do to help with situations like that?

Did Jesus break any rules? Did He say why, if He did break some?

Activity: One of the most effective ways to counter self-focus is by serving others. Set up a regular time to help at a homeless kitchen, volunteer at a thrift store run by a charity, or visit lonely people in nursing homes. You might think your teen's (and your) schedule is too busy to take on service of others. (That should be a red flag for you personally. Just sayin'.) And your attitude of either martyrdom and annoyance or joy in serving will rub off. It will also give you a chance to discuss with your teen the outcome of lives spent in addictions of all sorts.

Discussion questions:

Did the service situation give you any insight into how people got into unfortunate experiences? For instance, did anyone you served talk about their circumstances or their history?

Did you observe anything that people you served seemed to have in common? What made each one different from the others? Different from you?

FIVE

You Want Me to Talk about S-E-X?

Cherie was excited when she finally got to high school and could perform in the marching band. Today the band teacher leads the group, with its drums and cymbals and tubas, out of the stadium where they usually practice, to a nearby neighborhood with a large park. The change of scenery is an adventure. As a unit, they are carried along by the pulsing, raucous rhythms, the staccato beat. Cherie's home faces this park, and as she eases into the cadences, she sees her house coming into view. It's as if she were seeing it for the first time.

She wonders what the others might think of her modest house. Would they see the bricks coming loose or her little sister's trike in the yard? How did it compare, she wonders for the first time, with other houses as seen by her bandmates' eyes? But feelings of comfort and welcome and peace fill her heart. High school is a little scary, and there are lots of people and ideas she doesn't really know what to think about. But this house is where she comes for answers, for hugs, and for the silly inside jokes of her family.

Marching near her is Jason, a neighbor and friend from her church's youth group. He is a year ahead of her in school, and he barely looks up at his own home as he marches by. He knows what it symbolizes: *Rules, rules, rules. Don't, don't, don't. Do as I say, not do as I do.* He loves the band and even puts up with school because that's where he goes every day to be with people who "get" him, who are like him even when they are different. He can discuss anything with his friends, and they don't judge. And come graduation, he'll leave his house in his dust. The real world is out here, not behind those walls.

Cherie sees another clarinet player, Julie, puffing to keep up. This morning, Julie's backpack spilled and out fell a magazine—actually, the most popular teen magazine in the world—with a cover story about anal sex. *Anal* Cherie understood. *Sex?* As she marches along, she remembers what Mom always says: "*You got questions? I won't be embarrassed. We'll figure it out together.*"

Cherie has a wave of sympathy for Julie. *Bet she doesn't have a mom who wouldn't be embarrassed to talk about that,* she thinks, and makes a mental note to ask when she gets home.

"It's my job to protect you," Cherie's mom, Sue, has told her several times.

Sue had to overcome the memory of her own home sex "education," which had amounted to brochures slipped to her as if they were contraband and never to be discussed.

Sue had vowed to make her sex-ed plan for her daughter "not just about STDs, pregnancy, and gender, but to let her know what the world can't teach—about how amazing God's plan is for sex."

Out of Your Comfort Zone?

Parents may not be aware, but sex education is already underway for most kids. The average age at which a boy first views internet porn is eleven.[1] By that tender age, kids probably already have some colorful ideas of what sex is about, and they're probably wrong. If their parents don't ever talk about sex—godly sex—it will never occur to them that sex has much to do with family life or faith.

Parents often talk around sex, but not directly about it. Unfortunately, almost every other source in your teen's life is actively describing and promoting promiscuity. Pornography is a billion-dollar business with people racking their brains 24/7 to figure out how to make your kid just as addicted to the world's view of sex as everyone else. You will have to be just as direct in promoting God's plan for sex.

I wish there were some activities to help parents be more comfortable having conversations with teens about sexuality. I don't think those magical activities exist; I think that for us to be comfortable talking about sex with teens, we have to be willing to talk about sex with our spouses and trusted friends and family members. But for most of us, even that will be hard.

Barriers to Dialoguing about Sex

- We don't have many—or any—role models for talking with teens about sex because for most of us, no adults talked to us about it, and if they did, it was pretty awkward.

- Many of us grew up in homes and churches where sex was discussed in terms of purity or marital fidelity. Those are legitimate and vital concepts, but using those as the limits of your conversation won't help your teen much. The concept of purity, for instance, may be incomprehensible. Today's teens are practically swimming in sexual references all around them. They need more information to counter what they're hearing and seeing.

- Many of us don't have good sexual knowledge ourselves. We struggle with sex in our own lives and aren't communicating with the people closest to us about it.
- Sexual discussions involve having an emotionally intimate conversation. Face it: Many of us are not naturally equipped to talk about sex as an emotionally intimate issue.
- We've gotten the impression that sex is embarrassing, even lewd. Discussing it seems like nasty talk. Nobody taught us that God likes sex, that He created sex to enhance intimacy, bonding, and communication in marriage.

Until we address and resolve our discomfort with these barriers, we aren't going to be effective in discussing sex with our teens. They may see the difficulties more clearly than we do. The best way to work through these barriers is to practice breaking the ice by having some frank and open discussions with our spouses, and perhaps with friends. For single parents, meeting with trusted friends and family members could help.

Brainstorm about this. One strategy is to choose a recently released movie to watch together that deals with teen sexuality (perhaps even one that glorifies premarital sex) and discuss it with your teens. (Your kids may be impressed that you know about the movie.) Another tactic would be to form a kind of task force with some friends and sit and read aloud the Song of Solomon, which is actually quite an erotic piece of literature about anticipation and married love. You can watch each other squirm and then discuss how to overcome any discomfort, and later discuss how some of the ideas in that scriptural passage might be conveyed to your kids.

Myth versus Reality

In addition to our personal discomfort when discussing sex, other things hinder how we discuss sex with kids and lure us into talking *around* sexual issues rather than addressing them directly.

MYTH	REALITY
Talking about specific sexual information will encourage teens to become sexually active.	If we don't talk about specific sexual information, all the information teens have will be from the media, peers, and the internet.
Talking about specific sexual information is impure.	God created us in His image and as sexual beings. Sex is part of His plan in creation.
Talking about specific sexual information will only encourage adolescents to be lewd, silly, and vulgar.	If we are comfortable and relevant in talking about sex, teens will be interested and respectful in their interactions.
Teaching teenagers to wait until marriage or to just say no is enough sex education.	In teaching teens to wait until marriage, we have inadvertently taught them that anything is acceptable except vaginal intercourse.
Talking about purity is talking about sex.	Talking about purity is too general for teens inundated with specific sexual messages every day. We can define purity for them in sexual terms.
Talking about STDs and pregnancy is talking about sex.	STDs and pregnancies are consequences of sex. If we don't talk about sex itself, discussions of STDs and pregnancies aren't meaningful to teens.

Teens tell me again and again that what we are saying when we talk about sex isn't connecting with what's going on in their world. Sex is a hush-hush, taboo subject in many churches—and in most families. John Delony, a relationship and emotional wellness advisor with the Dave Ramsey organization and a former college administrator, writes,

> A common situation may look like this: A 9th grade girl falls head-over-heels for a 10th grade boy. He introduces her to kissing, touching and making out, and increasingly sexualized behavior. She is surprised to discover that making out feels good yet shameful, and that she likes feeling desired. She is left alone to untangle her mixed-feelings about physical intimacy, her first romantic feelings, ill-defined no-sex-before-marriage expectations, and her deep desire to be loved, included, and connected. On the other hand, the boy hasn't heard anything about sex from his church, his youth minister, or his parents beyond a blanket "Don't." With no tools or invitations to approach adults with deeper questions, he turns to the internet, other teens, and pornography for advice, instructional how-to's, and his first models for what sex and intimacy looks like. This is a recipe for disaster. Both teens want to feel loved and connected and are desperate for models of healthy sex and intimacy. Unfortunately, the grown-ups in their life remain silent and the teens are left getting their information from other teenagers or distorted sexualized messages on the internet.[2]

Teens need someone to talk with them about what to expect in a sexual relationship in marriage. They yearn for someone to have a frank, honest discussion with them about boundaries in a dating relationship.

Teens want us to use the real words and have real information for them. We need to be able to use relatively current terms that are nonmedical and non-vulgar for genitalia and sexual activities. Teens hear daily about orgasm, masturbation, oral sex, anal sex, and erections on television, online, in school, and from friends. They aren't going to view us as a credible information source if we can't even use those sexual terms in a conversation.

The Right Thing to Say

Your teens need to know you love them and care about what's important to them. Listen, but listen wisely: Discussions concerning sex should not become extended conversations where teens recount sexual escapades (of their own or others). Instead, after initially disclosing a sexual issue, the conversations need to be about changing the inappropriate behavior.

I counsel kids all the time about sexual issues. Though they may not say these words out loud, here are the messages they are sending their parents:

Are you actually listening to me? Listening to teens—about anything that interests and concerns them—will strengthen our relationship with them and make it more likely they will talk to us about sex and other personal issues.

Don't force me to say I'm wrong. We get much further in conversations if we don't try to wrangle them into agreement. Give them time to come around.

Be straight with me. We gain major points for credibility with teens when they know we will be honest and direct in our communication. Teens may not like what we say, but if we are providing factual, truthful information, they respect it. That does not mean that we make accusations or value statements. We share factual information.

Tell me you understand. Teens feel understood when we reflect their feelings back to them (e.g., "What I hear you saying is . . .") and recognize that feelings are a major aspect of sexual decisions. (Think back to your own teen years. Weren't there times you simply couldn't think straight because you were sexually distracted?) Acknowledging their emotional responses does not mean that we approve of their behaviors. It simply means we are responsive to their reactions to situations.

Give me a safe place to talk. Make them feel safe with your genuine interest in what concerns them, and with your supportiveness of their sharing. Tell them up front that we will only disclose information when they or someone they know is not safe, but outside of that we will maintain confidentiality. We won't tell our friends or family members what they tell us. We will not gossip about what they tell us, even disguised as vague "prayer requests." If things seem to be beyond your capability to help, tell them you will only ask for help from someone who will also keep your teen's confidence.

Get it right. Check back with them to make sure we have gotten all the factual information correct and that we have gotten all the relevant information in the situation.

Help me get a handle on what's right. Teens are searching for standards defining right and wrong. They can't reach for those standards if they don't know what they are! Ask teens what they think you would do in that situation. (The popular question "What would Jesus do?" is an unattainable standard for many teens.) Let them borrow your conscience.

"But everyone else is doing it." When teens use this statement to justify their behavior, gently remind them that you are concerned about them, not about everyone else. Reinforce that they are children of God. Talk about their behavior, not everyone else's behavior. If they continue to bring up other people's behavior, remind them that you are talking to them, not everyone else.

Talk about the tough stuff. When teens start talking about troubling personal issues, don't avoid the subject. If teens reveal an issue that you don't have the skills to handle, assure them that you hear what they are telling you and that you will find someone who can help them. Then go find someone who can help them!

What do you think of me now? If teens reveal that they have been engaged in sexual behavior, reassure them that you care about them and emphasize that you still see them as a child of God. Don't condone the behavior, but assure teens that they can change that behavior and find forgiveness in their relationship with God.[3]

Conversation Killers

I can't believe you did that. Teens who made a mistake don't go to a parent for commentary on what they did. They probably already have a pretty good idea of how they got into the mess; now they need help dealing with the consequences of a poor decision. An emotional reaction—"I can't believe you did that!"—isn't going to build bridges and will likely shut down communication between you and your teen.

Not my problem. True, technically it may not be your immediate problem. But if we don't help them with the problem, teens aren't going to make better choices. And they'll make those decisions without our presence and communication.

Let me tell you about . . . Jumping in with a story about someone with similar issues is not going to help teens. They don't want to know about other people, they want help with their own current situation.

Here's what you should do. Although we may clearly see an effective way to handle a situation, teens usually don't want someone to just tell them what to do. They will welcome Mom or Dad helping them brainstorm a way to solve their own problems.

Final Thoughts

Your plan for talking to your teen about sex needs to start with your being comfortable—and making your teen at least receptive with your relaxed attitude. You, more than anyone in the world, can give them confidence that they will be able to deal with their sexual desires in a godly manner; you will be an anchor of hope that will help them emerge from adolescence with a healthy view of sex in marriage and healthy boundaries to deal with sexual temptation outside of marriage. If we don't know their struggles and their stories, we can't meet them where they are and help them develop a godly understanding of sexuality.

It may surprise your teen to know that God talked about sex a lot in the Bible—not just the "thou shalt nots" and mistakes people made, but in positive ways that encourage marital intimacy. The Bible even tells husbands and wives to have sex regularly. (What? A "thou *shalt* have sex" commandment? Several of them. You didn't know that either? Read on!)

Like many changes in behavior, new attitudes about faith and sex will usually require talking through first.

But be aware that discussions don't always bear fruit right away. And the power of words is a double-edged sword: "With the tongue we praise our Lord and Father, and with it we curse human beings, who have been made in God's likeness. Out of the same mouth come praise and cursing" (James 3:9–10).

The problem is that even though God talked about sex often, we probably don't. We might think that talking about sex is nasty (see James's statement above), but God doesn't think sex is nasty at all. It was His idea to begin with.

EXPLORATION
WITH YOUR TEEN

Sometimes a natural conversation opener will come when discussing media or friends. Here are some suggestions:

Comment from teen: "I don't really want to talk about sex" (with you, right now, etc.).

Parent answer: "I can understand that. I think a lot of teens feel that way, like maybe talking about it might be kind of awkward. But it's my job to see that you get accurate information about sex—so aren't there any questions you have about sex that I might help you with? And if I don't know the answer, I'll do some research for you."

Question from a parent: "Did you know the Bible commands people to have sex?"
Some Scriptures to look up with your teen:

And God blessed them. And God said to them, "Be fruitful and multiply and fill the earth and subdue it, and have dominion over the fish of the sea and over the birds of the heavens and over every living thing that moves on the earth."

Genesis 1:28 ESV

The husband should give to his wife her conjugal rights, and likewise the wife to her husband. For the wife does not have authority over her own body, but the husband does. Likewise the husband does not have authority over his own body, but the wife does. Do not deprive one another, except perhaps by agreement for a limited time, that you may devote yourselves to prayer; but then come together again, so that Satan may not tempt you because of your lack of self-control.

1 Corinthians 7:3–5 ESV

Let your fountain be blessed,
     and rejoice in the wife of your youth,
     a lovely deer, a graceful doe.
Let her breasts fill you at all times with delight;
     be intoxicated always in her love.

Proverbs 5:18–19 ESV

Question from a parent: Did you know there's a whole book of the Bible about sexual attraction, and it's all positive? (Read with your teen a section you have preselected from Song of Solomon chapter 1 or 2.)

It's important that you review Foundational Issue #2: What It Means to Be a Human, from chapter 2, and make sure you're firm on the biblical teaching that human beings are body plus soul. You will have to keep that in mind and be able to explain it so your teen will understand. It's a nonthreatening way to introduce sexual issues by talking generally about the body and its relationship to the soul.

As an exercise, ask yourself: Which sexual issues are most difficult for you to discuss with your teens? What strategies can you use to prepare to discuss them? A possible solution might be to seek the advice of friends who have raised godly children. Without meaning to sound unkind, I don't advise you to seek the sadder-but-wiser counsel of those who weren't able to do that.

Activity: My coauthor, Dr. Scott, found some sexual discussion engendered by reading a chronological Bible aloud with her son (she used *The Daily Bible*, and she read the introductory and explanatory sections each day while her son read the text, over about a two-year period). The Bible is quite unabashed about arousal, sexual self-control, and even controversial and timely subjects that range from incest and rape to the withdrawal method of birth control. And after all, if God is talking about it, it's okay for you to, and it can open doors for you to talk about it later with questions such as, "Did you understand what was going on there?"

SIX

Intimacy and Boundaries

When Amanda's parents came to me, they were full of questions, second-guessing all of their parenting decisions. Sixteen-year-old Amanda, an outstanding volleyball player, proclaimed to be a lesbian and in love with a teammate.

Taking Amanda off the team wasn't the right solution, so they talked to their youth minister and then made an appointment with me. I talked with them and Amanda, and then had a session with Amanda alone. She is a kind-natured, sensitive person whose demeanor in private doesn't match the killer athlete I know her to be. Then I asked the question nobody had posed to her before.

"*Why* do you think you are lesbian?"

"I love Katelyn," she says. "I've never felt this way about anyone else before. I can tell her anything and she understands it. She really gets me."

"So when did you first realize you were interested in Katelyn in a sexual way?"

Amanda looks a little puzzled. "I'm not sure."

Now I am a little puzzled. "When you told me that you were a lesbian, I assumed that you were involved sexually with another female."

"Oh! I haven't done anything sexual with Katelyn," Amanda tells me. "I love her, but we haven't really done anything like, like *that*. We've slept in the same bed and snuggled, but nothing beyond that."

"So you think you are a lesbian because you love Katelyn?"

"Yes. We have such a connection. She gets what I am feeling and thinking before I even tell her."

"Has Katelyn been involved with other females in the past?"

"No, this is the first time either one of us have felt this way."

"I recognize that you feel emotionally connected to Katelyn, but being a lesbian involves more than emotional intimacy. Being a lesbian means that you are sexually attracted to Katelyn."

Amanda shrugs. "I guess I hadn't really thought about whether I'm sexually attracted to Katelyn and whether she is sexually attracted to me."

"Let's talk about the different types of intimacy," I say. "Did you know you can be intimate with someone without it being sexual?"

After a discussion about different types of intimacy, I asked Amanda to share that information with Katelyn, and asked if her friend would meet with us both. When we met the next time, we discussed the types of intimacy in relationships, including intellectual intimacy, emotional intimacy, physical intimacy, spiritual intimacy, and sexual intimacy. After our discussion, both Amanda and Katelyn agreed that they were emotionally and spiritually intimate, but that they were not lesbians. Several years later, they were attendants in each other's weddings, and they continue to be lifelong friends.

Unfortunately, when people today talk about intimacy in a relationship, we often equate it to sexual intimacy. In our culture, we seem to have blurred the boundaries between different types of intimacy and have lumped all intimacy in relationships into sexual intimacy. But sex is just one form of intimacy. Intimacy is a process that leads to feeling as though we are truly seen and known by someone else. As intimacy grows stronger, we feel a stronger connection to the other person.

There are two very significant examples in the Bible of same-sex relationships that were intimate but not sexual. The first is the friendship of David and Jonathan. It was risky for Jonathan; he and David both knew that if David rose to power, he would displace Jonathan as the heir apparent to the throne of Israel. It was further complicated because Jonathan's father, King Saul, actually threatened David's life. But Jonathan's deep love for his friend was more important to him than his own future. Jonathan took risk after risk to protect his friend. And we can see the profound effect of that kind of friendship in what David said about Jonathan when his beloved friend was killed in battle:

> I grieve for you, Jonathan my brother;
>> you were very dear to me.
> Your love for me was wonderful,
>> more wonderful than that of women.
>
> 2 Samuel 1:26

With that, David set the bar high for pure, self-sacrificial, intimate relationships between men. This is echoed in the New Testament with the tenderness and affection in relationships of men like Paul and Timothy.

Similarly, two women in the Bible showed dedication and intimate love—and where we in our culture would find it most unusual: between a mother-in-law and daughter-in-law! Both widows and at the point of starvation, Ruth and Naomi became traveling companions who wouldn't give up on each other. "But Ruth replied, 'Don't urge me to leave you or to turn back from you. Where you go I will go, and where you stay I will stay. Your people will be my people and your God my God. Where you die I will die, and there I will be buried. May the LORD deal with me, be it ever so severely, if even death separates you and me'" (Ruth 1:16–17). At the risk of their own lives, they protected each other with deep and intimate love.

Our culture has robbed us of the high calling of deep, intimate relationships that don't involve sex. Whereas two men or two women of the past could work side by side as missionaries or traveling companions or even housemates, now there is the accusation of homosexuality lurking nearby. What an enormous loss for us.

In fact, the Bible shows that we can have tender and emotionally intimate relationships if we view each other as treasured parents and siblings. There are of course boundaries whether the relationships are same-sex or between male and female, but those boundaries can still encompass great affection.

Treat "older women as mothers, and younger women as sisters, with absolute purity," Paul instructs Timothy (1 Timothy 5:2). "It's like he's saying, 'Think about your own sisters and extend that very same level of love and purity to the young women in your church.'"[1]

Types of Intimacy

We understand the irreplaceable value of a bestie, of intimacy that will never lead to a sexual relationship, and we can help our kids understand that too. After all, our craving for intimacy mirrors the fervent relationship God wants to have with individuals. He understands this very well, and in sympathy and love created Eve for Adam after stating that it's not good for humans to be alone. Experiencing intellectual intimacy, emotional intimacy, and spiritual intimacy in our friendships equips us to develop more intimacy in our romantic relationships, and more commitment and faithfulness to friends. Your teens need to know this applies throughout their lifetime.

Aside from sexual intimacy, the four other main types of intimacy help define relationships that help teens grow as Christians.

Emotional Intimacy

Emotional intimacy means that you can talk to someone about your innermost feelings. You can share your joy, cry with their pain, and laugh with their happiness. You allow yourself to be vulnerable, sharing your feelings and taking the risk of rejection from your friend.

When teens are reaching out to develop relationships outside the family, they are greatly moved by an emotional connection with another person. This acceptance by a non-family member often helps when teens are struggling with anxiety or depression. They may feel like they are heard or understood for the first time, and they may be willing to share feelings they have not shared before. Sometimes sharing secret emotional events from their life can cement that emotional connection with a peer.

Intellectual Intimacy

Intellectual intimacy includes sharing ideas and thoughts about what is important to you. It deepens when teens find delight in someone who shares the same favorite songs, poems, books, or videos. Even though they may not have identical tastes, teens enjoy watching movies or reading books they can share their perceptions about. When commonalities emerge, they share dreams and plans for the future, discussing travel, college plans, or dreams about marriage.

Physical Intimacy

Physical intimacy is not the same as sexual intimacy. It's essentially being affectionate with each other, which can include everything from hugging to holding hands to cuddling on the couch. Physical intimacy is the type of physical contact parents have with their children. As children become teens, they may become more resistant to physical contact with their parents and begin seeking it in relationships with peers. Among males, the desire for physical contact may manifest itself as wrestling and play activities while females are generally more comfortable with hugs and such.

Spiritual Intimacy

Spiritual intimacy is sharing about your relationship with God. It may include praying together, reading the Bible together, and/or "God talk"—sharing what is happening with your relationship with God and listening to a peer do the same. Christian kids often share testimonies they have heard, or faith-building facts about creation or other aspects of nature. With spiritual intimacy, you are able to be open and honest with each other and to listen to what the other person is saying, trying to understand where the other person is coming from and how you can nurture each other's relationships with the divine.

Each teen may respond differently to the various types of intimacy. But knowing about each kind, and how they differ in nature and purpose from sexual intimacy, is a conversation you need to have with your teen. It may not have occurred to them, as it did not to Amanda, that intimacy doesn't have to equal sex, and that the world's definitions of relationships may be just flat-out wrong.

Boundaries: To Restrict or to Protect?

In contrast to my meetings with Amanda and her good friend Katelyn is the story of Elisha. When I met her, she was struggling with drug use and was heavily involved in violent sexual activities with multiple male and female partners. She had no sense of boundaries about her sexual activities. Her parents and youth workers were stunned when as a young adult she dropped out of church and moved in with a drug dealer. They were unaware of her history of sexual activities and drug use.

Elisha's story illustrates the difficulty teens have in establishing sexual boundaries. Initially, Elisha was an observer of sexual activity who agreed to keep a secret. Soon she became a participant, and then began experimenting with all types of sexual activity. Her heartrending life illustrates how crossing one boundary leads to crossing more: Getting to where she ended up, in sexual activities with multiple partners, was a gradual process.

Our culture tells teens that rules are made to be broken and that boundaries (except for a few politically correct ones) are irrelevant. That's because they see boundaries as restrictive and not as protective.

God himself sets boundaries, and every human on earth owes Him for that! For instance, He set limits on how far the oceans can encroach on land.[2] On those remarkable times that a tsunami, for instance, rolls past those limits, we remember how grateful we are for God's boundaries! In the garden of Eden, God gave Adam and Eve access to every life-giving tree and restricted them only from the one that could bring death into the world. And in a society of scarce court proceedings, He even established whole cities where people accused of crimes could go and safely wait until their case was decided.[3]

God is all about boundaries—restrictions that are designed to protect. As parents, you set boundaries so your kids don't touch hot stoves, cross streets alone, or get in cars with strangers. Your teen would do the same when baby-sitting little kids. This is a good analogy to share with your teen to show that older people know about some kinds of dangers before younger people are aware of the consequences and implications.

Inevitably, a discussion of sexual boundaries seems to revolve around the question of how far is far enough. Too often our answers are vague generalities like "It's different for everyone" and "You'll know when you've gone too far." The problem with these generalities is that teens do indeed have to go "too far" to find out what *too far* is. We are actually teaching "Stop, don't stop, stop." We are saying don't have sex, just go far enough to know what is too far, then don't do it.

When teens realize they've gone too far, you can offer hope and help, but know that they have removed a boundary that is difficult to rebuild. Once you cross over by violating a dearly held belief—what some call a "bright line" or clear boundary, aka the level ground in absolutely any aspect of life—everything gets muddy and harder. That's just rock-hard reality your kid needs to know.

But surprise! Many kids *aren't violating their consciences* with oral sex or other behaviors because they don't think such things are wrong. How much better to talk to your teen and establish what the Bible teaches about godly sexual behavior instead of seeing your kid struggle with climbing back up from falling over a line they never understood was there and then dealing with the physical, emotional, and spiritual consequences.

The concept of sexual boundaries is almost taboo in a society that has few taboos. Our culture teaches that sex defines almost all relationships. Sex defines happiness. Sex is the key to fulfillment and success. Sex will sell a product when nothing else will. Who you are sexually in our society is who you are period. Our challenge is to help teens define their identity in a relationship with God rather than buying in to the illusion that sex defines identity.

What Is Sex?

To have an accurate, godly perspective about sex, we have to define sex. Traditionally, we have told teens "Don't do it," but we haven't defined "it." If we define "it" as intercourse, we may be inadvertently giving teens permission to engage in any sexual activity that is not intercourse. But, of course, intercourse is a culminating event in the process we could call sex.

What is sex?

- Everything leading up to or resulting from intercourse.
- Everything we see or touch that stimulates sexual arousal.
- Sexual thoughts, the longing to unite, the emotional commitment.
- Passionate kisses, heavy petting, and foreplay.
- Pornography, explicit fantasy, and self-arousal.
- An internal process leading up to sexual arousal.
- Anything that has the potential to result in intercourse or masturbation.[4]

Once sex is defined as a process, it is easier to help teens begin to consider boundaries for sexual activity. When teens ask, "How far is too far?" they may be asking for information they don't know about the process of sexual behavior. Teens who don't recognize anything except intercourse as sex won't see anything wrong—and will see a lot good!—in engaging in other sexual behaviors.

Typically, teens get plenty of information about reproduction, but not information about sexual behaviors leading up to intercourse. In fact, teens may have more information about the consequences of sex (pregnancy and STDs) than they have about sex itself.[5] Here's a useful chart about the physical continuum of sexual behavior.

Continuum of Sexual Behavior[6]

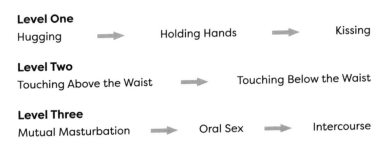

Level One
Hugging ➡ Holding Hands ➡ Kissing

Level Two
Touching Above the Waist ➡ Touching Below the Waist

Level Three
Mutual Masturbation ➡ Oral Sex ➡ Intercourse

Don't let your teen tell you they can't understand boundaries in sexual relationships. A marriage is a sexual relationship, so ask your teen to imagine that their mother is married and has taken a new job. Since she has started her new job, she has developed a personal relationship with her boss, an attractive and charismatic man who is slightly younger than she is. Mom and her boss have begun to spend more time together. They frequently work on the same projects and attend luncheon meetings together. Some weekends they work on projects. Using the continuum of sexual behavior above, ask teens:

"Would it be okay for Mom to kiss her boss?"

"Hold his hand?"

"Hug him?"

Teens are usually quick to say that no physical contact is appropriate. If teens can so easily define appropriate boundaries for a sexual relationship within a marriage, they can also hash out with you some of the admittedly looser appropriate boundaries for sexual relationships outside of marriage.

Obviously and appropriately, teens have sexual thoughts and urges because they are experiencing puberty and because God created all of us as sexual beings. The challenge is to help teens distinguish between having normal sexual urges and thoughts and becoming involved in sexual behaviors that are only appropriate in a marital relationship.

Teens are likely to view a sexual continuum quite differently and argue,

- "You aren't having sex if you wear a condom."
- "You aren't having sex if you don't have an orgasm during intercourse."
- "Oral sex isn't sex."
- "Anything that doesn't lead to having a baby isn't sex."

A generation or two ago, teens understood sexual boundaries as progressive and talked about getting to first base, second base, or third base before getting a home run (intercourse). Today's youth don't recognize a progression. They see two categories: intercourse, which they would say is sex, and everything else, which is not sex. In fact, many teens would view holding hands and oral sex as being equally intimate and permissible. In our society, oral sex is a sometimes-preferred sexual activity for teens who believe it is without risk, thinking they can't get pregnant and they can't get STDs from oral sex (though of course they can catch STDs through oral sex).

Your teen may already be involved in fondling, mutual masturbation, and oral sex. It may be difficult to persuade these teens that their current behavior is inappropriate sexual contact outside the confines of a marriage. A Christian teen may believe that stopping short of intercourse is exercising self-control and might be surprised that a parent wouldn't take that into account and give them credit for it. Even if we convince these teens that their behavior is inappropriate, it will be a struggle for them to change their sexual boundaries in dating relationships.

Spiritual and Emotional Consequences

An understanding of the physical continuum isn't enough. They may suspect this already, but you must tell them there are emotional and spiritual consequences of sexual behavior. Moving past hugging and kissing into more sexual behavior creates an emotional bond. Sex connects people in a way nothing else can.

During intercourse, a female releases a powerful hormonal chemical called oxytocin (often called "the attachment hormone"), which creates in her what one sex therapist calls "an involuntary chemical commitment,"[7] whether she intends it or not. For males, vasopressin creates the urge to bond. This is all designed by God to strengthen commitment in marriage, and thus sex outside of marriage is extremely confusing to the human body and mind, especially to adolescents.

Any sexual activity requires trust, to some degree, on the part of both people, because sexual activities inherently create vulnerability. Such closeness leads couples to make decisions about their relationship based on a connection found in sex rather than making decisions based on their relationship with God.

Teens who have sex with multiple partners will argue that for them, sex doesn't create a bond between them and their sexual partners. But if teens have reached the point where sex does not create a bond with their sexual partner, it means they have lost their ability to trust and be vulnerable in a sexual relationship. They will seek to maintain as much control as possible in any sexual encounter. I've seen it over and over in my counseling practice: Teens who have lost this ability to trust in a sexual relationship frequently begin to use drugs, mutilate themselves, and take risks with their lives because sex isn't fulfilling their need for acceptance and intimacy. Their emotional and spiritual isolation makes them seek out sexual behaviors they think *won't* produce intimacy.

Teens who choose intimate sexual contact outside of marriage experience spiritual consequences. More and more frequently, teens tell me that they are sexually active because it feels good. It's shocking for parents to realize their teens are worshiping sexual pleasure rather than worshiping God, choosing their own physical pleasure over their relationship with God. Similarly, teens who are seeking emotional acceptance and fulfillment through a sexual relationship are looking in the wrong place to have their needs met. These teens are engaging in sexual behavior because they want to be loved. They are choosing an imitation of love rather than choosing the love that God offers them.

Warning: No Relationship Required

Today, teens may engage in sexual activities without having an emotional or dating relationship with their sexual partners. As parents, we need to realize that dating relationships are not required for sexual activity. Teens may have "friends with benefits" or even speak of "situationships" instead of relationships. Sexual liaisons are to them like sampling foods at Costco: You can see how it tastes but you don't have to invest in it even if you like it. Just come up the aisle again and get another sample.

If you're a teen soaking up media depictions of situationships, it may be a mental reach to even envision any long-term relationship, much less a marriage. Sex is what you do with your body, teens might say. (See the separation of body and spirit showing up here again?) As difficult as it is for us to comprehend, teens may view sexual activity as nothing more than a physical event that requires some precautions so nobody gets hurt.

How Do We Help Teens Set Boundaries?

- *Talk about sex as a process*, not as a culminating event with various types of escalating sexual activity. Since

it's a process, engaging in one type of behavior can lead
to another behavior. The challenge is to decide what
limits will stop the process.

- *Go counterculture.* Look at ads on television and online
  and ask your teen to see the ways our culture is selling
  sex as the integral component of identity. Is sex who we
  are? Or does God say something else?

- *Set "bright lines" (unambiguous and nonnegotiable
  rules) of expectation.* Be willing to say to teens that
  sexual behaviors are wrong and hold them accountable for changing their behavior. After counseling with
  thousands of teens, I can tell you that they don't want
  us to endorse their behavior. They want us to teach
  them right from wrong and to confront them when
  they are involved in sexual behavior. They want and
  need to know their boundaries are not to restrict but to
  protect.

- *Encourage group activities.* This means you may have
  to be inconvenienced by opening up your home for
  movies or parties. You may have to strategize and
  plan with other parents. You will have to give up
  some of your evenings or weekends to be a chaper-
  one, and to think about how to do that in a fun way.
  Keep in mind that teen couples who are allowed to
  spend a lot of time alone together are going to be
  tempted to engage in sexual behavior, so they'll need
  alternatives. Don't let teens wander off by themselves
  during youth group activities or have exclusive time
  alone with peers on overnight activities or out-of-
  town trips.

- Talk to your teen about why it's important to avoid
  sexual experimentation and to wait until marriage to
  engage in sexual behaviors. Discuss God's plan for sex

and help your teen view waiting as a smart, worthwhile decision to at least delay and perhaps even sacrifice their own feelings and desires to a higher purpose—which is to glorify Him.

- *Use the swimming suit rule*: Your teen doesn't touch anyone or allow anyone to touch them in areas covered by a swimming suit.

- *Horizontal is bad.* Nothing good happens when two teens are lying down.

- *Magnify grace.* Help teens engaging in sexual behavior to realize that God will forgive them. Show them that 1 John 1:7 tells us to turn our face to the light, to walk in it. And the cleansing action of God is like a windshield wiper, continuously forgiving as we try to obey.

- *Actions are measurable but worth isn't.* Try this exercise with your teen: Brainstorm about how far you can go in doing something good (as opposed to how far you can go without sinning). You are just as valuable a human being with either course of action—but walking a tightrope of sexual appropriateness is exhausting.

Final Thoughts: Drugs and Alcohol

Having an undeveloped brain is one challenge for teens. It's made worse by drinking and using drugs, which reduce inhibitions and a teen's ability to make good decisions. Their bright lines become dim. When teens drink or use drugs, they have a distorted sense of their surroundings, are unable to set clear sexual boundaries, and may not recognize dangerous situations. Quite literally, being intoxicated or high may reduce a teen's ability to physically or verbally resist sex.

Teach your teen to avoid attending activities where others are using drugs and alcohol. Some situations will have more obvious drug or alcohol use than others. Help your teen to realize that having adult chaperones is for their safety. In addition, teens need to avoid parties with teens they don't know and not accept food or drinks from people they don't know. According to Alcohol.org, 56 percent of women report having had their drinks spiked; more than half of these spiking situations took place while respondents were in college, and 19 percent happened to participants in high school.[8]

EXPLORATION
WITH YOUR TEEN

Read the story of how David and Jonathan's friendship began right after David killed Goliath:

> After David had finished talking with Saul, Jonathan became one in spirit with David, and he loved him as himself. From that day Saul kept David with him and did not let him return home to his family. And Jonathan made a covenant with David because he loved him as himself. Jonathan took off the robe he was wearing and gave it to David, along with his tunic, and even his sword, his bow and his belt.
>
> 1 Samuel 18:1–4

Ask your teen, What tells you that these men had a true friendship?

Since the Jewish law condemned homosexuality (Leviticus), and this friendship is approved in the Bible, how do we know it was intimate but not sexual? Which of the four types of intimacy do we see here?

Jonathan later put his own life at risk to keep David safe. Read about the details in 1 Samuel 20. What do you see in the story of David and Jonathan that reminds you of John 15:13?

Teens need help in establishing boundaries about sexual contact. You'll need to be creative if they're not inclined to discuss it.

1. Jesus had close, intimate, and appropriate relationships (with Peter, James, John, Lazarus, Mary, and Martha, among others). However, even He had boundaries, because He knew all trust of human beings has limits. Read John 2:23–25 and discuss this with your teen.

   > Now while he was in Jerusalem at the Passover Festival, many people saw the signs he was performing and believed in his name. But Jesus would not entrust himself to them, for he knew all people. He did not need any testimony about mankind, for he knew what was in each person.

2. God set boundaries in the physical world. Discuss Job 38:8–11 with your teen and ask, "Do water molecules, doing what's 'natural,' know what's best for them? For human beings? How do the boundaries of a Creator show love? How does a limit show protection?"

   > (God speaking):
   >
   > Who shut up the sea behind doors
   >   when it burst forth from the womb,
   > when I made the clouds its garment
   >   and wrapped it in thick darkness,
   > when I fixed limits for it
   >   and set its doors and bars in place,
   > when I said, "This far you may come and no farther;
   >   here is where your proud waves halt"?

3. Brainstorm with your teen about how talking up front about boundaries and limits up front in a dating situation, for instance, helps prevent undesirable outcomes. Young men, in particular, must have in mind clear definitions of what they will or will not initiate.

SEVEN

Understanding Relationships

Joe, Michael, and LeRoy

Joe doesn't really know what to tell his thirteen-year-old daughter about dating. When Joe was just entering his own teenage years, his parents read books like *I Kissed Dating Goodbye* and decided that Joe would pursue a future mate through courtship: His parents would participate in the selection of his future wife, and all contact between the two young people would be with the intention of an eventual marriage.

"I had my moments," Joe says about some covert sexual experimentation that involved kissing and fondling girls that his parents would have called "the wrong kind of girls," but in the end, his parents guided him in courting. Once Joe began obediently (and enthusiastically) pursuing pretty Julie with the aim of marrying her, the trajectory was set. Now, twenty years later, Joe and Julie have a stable marriage but are very much aware their daughter, Riordan, is unlikely to submit to the rigorous rules of courtship. In fact, Riordan, like many of her friends, isn't particularly interested in marriage at all, and certainly not in a process that would exclude her getting to know a lot of guys she's acquainted with. And when she gets to college, Joe and Julie are pretty sure any talk of a courtship like that of her parents will go out the window.

Joe goes to the gym with LeRoy and Michael, all three buddies since grade school. They talk about the challenges of raising their children.

Michael didn't become a Christian until his college years when LeRoy baptized him, but by that time Michael was quite experienced sexually and ended up marrying the college freshman he'd gotten pregnant. Now Michael is divorced and shares custody of two teenage sons. He very much wants to help them avoid his mistakes of "sowing wild oats."

For his part, LeRoy's parents had him participate in a "purity pledge" when he was twelve, and LeRoy felt terrible after sexual behavior that had stopped just short of intercourse. From that point on he managed to hold on to abstinence until he met his future wife, Lorraine, a virgin. LeRoy had been told that if you waited for intercourse until marriage, it would be the most terrific high-octane sex ever. To his and Lorraine's disappointment, sex was at first awkward and even painful for her before becoming more satisfying and unifying. It never approached the fireworks they'd been promised, "but we do have three great kids," LeRoy says.

The three men agree: They don't want to make guarantees or threats or even unkeepable rules. They know they want their kids to stay sexually pure. They know they don't want the girls to get pregnant, their sons to get a girl pregnant, or any of their children to contract a sexually transmitted disease. They want to keep their kids from guilt and unhappiness.

Joe won't tell his daughter that courtship is the only biblical way to choose a mate, even though it had a good result for him and Julie. When Riordan asked about it, "I told her it was something described in ancient biblical culture, but never commanded," he says. "So I'm not going to put my daughter through that."

Michael regrets what the kids would call his many "hook-ups" with past sexual partners, and is paying the price for what he calls "falling out of lust" with his ex-wife, who left him for a woman.

And LeRoy wants to take all the good things about the purity pledge without making unsustainable promises about the future as a reward for abstinence.

All three men know that things often don't work out the way you thought they would. But all three want to be men of faith and to help their children be men and women of faith.

It's a Brave New World

These dads have only an inkling of how much the landscape has changed for teenagers. Only 35 percent of American teens ages thirteen to seventeen have ever "dated, hooked up with or been otherwise romantically involved with another person," and only 18 percent are in a romantic relationship currently; most teens with dating experience (76 percent) say they have dated only people they met offline, despite the major role that technology plays in teen relationships.[1]

Texting is the top method of communication with a romantic partner, say teens (92 percent), but phone calling (87 percent) and in-person time (86 percent) combine with other digital ways to stay in touch.[2]

Imagine! Face-to-face meetings are not their preferred way of sharing thoughts!

Technology itself is a kind of group activity for teens who are dating—70 percent spend time together posting on social media sites and with their significant other using instant or online messaging. In addition, teens who are dating use video chat, messaging apps, and email.[3]

Teens also use social media "to express public support or approval of others' romantic relationships,"[4] with nearly two-thirds (63 percent) of teens with dating experience having posted or "liked" something to indicate their support of a friend's relationship. Girls are especially likely to do this: 71 percent of girls with dating experience have done so, compared with 57 percent of boys.

But even as they use social media to display their own relationships and support those of their friends, many teen daters hate being the subject of that kind of online attention: "Some 69% of teen social media users with dating experience agree that too many people can see what's happening in their relationship on social media; 16% of this group 'strongly' agrees."[5]

Not all the rules have changed: Almost half of girls still wait for boys—47 percent wait for the guy to initiate contact compared to only 6 percent of boys who wait for the girl.[6]

So maybe all this once-removed relationship stuff is okay, you might be thinking. A recent Centers for Disease Control and Prevention study did find that 45 percent of U.S. teenagers had never had intercourse by the time they reached age eighteen.[7] Finally! A note of hope! Many parents are reading this and thinking, *Whew! We've got about a 50/50 chance of getting my kid through high school without having sex.*

This might be good news to some Christian parents, the Joes and Michaels and LeRoys who, between them, went through the spectrum of dating in their own youth.

But the factors that have led young people to this kind of disconnect with sex are not good news at all.

One factor is teenage boys' use of porn (we'll discuss this in chapter 10), which not only substitutes for physical sex but also creates a mental ideal that real young women can hardly (nor should they) achieve.

Just as significant as porn, though, is the logical extension of the pervasive cultural thinking that sex is something you do with your body, detached from any true emotional or moral significance, and only important because of its potential for responsibilities (including messy breakups) and dangers (such as pregnancy and disease).

Teaching Teens about Dating

There's another high cost to tech-saturated relationships. Teens may know all the latest acronyms and emojis but often have no sense of social and relationship skills, which past generations caught from their culture or were taught by others. A particularly poignant example of this occurred when author Nancy Pearcey was approached after a college lecture by a group of students who asked her to teach them how to date. She suggests that "Christians need to start their own 'Go On a Date' courses for singles who have lost the art of dating."[8] One of the features I think would be essential in any such training would be to teach kids what healthy relationships look like. If Pearcey's observation and my own are accurate, most teens don't have a clue unless someone teaches them. Here are some suggestions:

1. A dating situation works best when each person takes delight in showing respect and deference to the other person.[9] After all, that's the Christian ideal, right? We don't check our Christianity at the door when we're trying to impress someone. You ask questions to get to know the other person and listen carefully to what they say. What makes them tick? You find out what they like, share what you like, and compromise by taking turns choosing activities. You show interest in their opinions, especially if they differ from yours, but you also feel free

to share what you think. Dating conversations should
be stimulating and peaceful at the same time.

2. You find ways to draw out the best in the other person. Give them opportunities to shine at what they do
well or share their accomplishments. Share what helps
you in your relationship with God and ask them the
same.

3. Other friends and other activities will continue to
be important. A date doesn't mean your life revolves
around the other person; that's too much pressure for
anyone. And most dates don't start a one-way trip to
marriage. Your relaxed attitude will rub off on the
other person, and you'll have a lot more fun!

Red Flags

Here's the other side of the coin you can discuss with your teen:
If "good" dating makes you a better person and closer to God,
and you learn how to compromise and have fun as you learn
about another person, what would be the signs of an unhealthy
relationship?

First, there's always a certain amount of nervousness when
you want to make a good impression, but constant fear, stress,
and sadness are not part of a healthy relationship. And it's good
to compromise on where to eat or what type of movie to go to,
but if you end up agreeing to do something you know is not
right, that's not compromise, it's coercion. And while a feeling
of guilt is appropriate when you've messed up, the motivation
for the guilt should come from your conscience, not from someone who is trying to make you feel guilty because you don't do
things their way.

Here are some other big red flags for unhealthy relationships. Discuss them with your teen ahead of time, because once

they're becoming attracted to someone, they may lose their sense of what's good and bad.

- Someone who wants to control the other or "needs" to know where they are every minute
- Possessiveness or jealousy. A dating partner may portray the other as just so irresistible that they can't do without them. But think about it: Your teen will tell you he or she deserves trust and independence from you, and they likewise need relationships with others who can similarly function independently.
- Feeling you're responsible when the other person messes up. (You "should be a better influence"?)
- Someone who says they need to reform you, or you need to reform them. (Leave that job to their mommies or parole officers.)
- Swearing, screaming, bullying, name-calling, pushing, shoving, hitting, sexual violence, or threats of any kind. **No. Not ever. Not even once.** Tell your teen you will come get him or her on a moment's notice and you will never ever blame your teen. You are their protector, and you're serious about your job.

The Mechanics of Dating

Tell your teen that when you operate on Jesus' Golden Rule to treat others as you want to be treated, a lot of the worries about dating diminish. You're less nervous when you are trying to make someone else comfortable.

You'll want to be your real self, so ask a person out who's likely to enjoy who you really are, not who you'd like to be—someone you have something in common with. You look past appearances and try to find good in others. You don't need to date everyone, but you can make everyone you date feel good about themselves. You can make things fun for them. You allow for their wants and needs and personality. You can be kind, no matter what.

Teens may need to be told some things you thought were just common sense.

- Put some planning into the date so that the person feels important being the point of such preparation. "Hanging out" can be relaxing and fun, but not all the time. Spontaneity is very appealing to some people but unnerving to others. And worst of all is boredom, which never ends well for anyone. Planning different and exciting activities for dates will keep things from getting awkward and tense. (You can help your teen brainstorm some fun date activities by searching the internet.)
- Smell your best. Look your best. Turn around in front of a full-length mirror before you go out the door. Females, lean forward to see how much you are exposing.
- Texting is fine, but signal to your date that this is something different by asking in person or calling to ask someone out on a date. That shows respect and courage.
- Make it your goal to help the other person have fun and feel good about your time together. Maybe write a prayer asking God's help for that.

This is just not natural behavior for today's teen. They'll need to practice. Do some role-playing and have your teen pretend to call and ask someone out. Have them role-play the "invitee" as well so they know how to accept or respectfully decline an invitation. Not all invitations should be accepted.

For teens to enjoy dating, they need to know how to eat in public. For instance, perhaps they shouldn't go to a spaghetti restaurant where the food is messy, or to a hibachi grill where they might singe their eyebrows off, as Dr. Scott's son did once on a memorable first date.

You'd think that popular movies would show people how to date, but most of them just portray any date-like situations as a prelude to sex. But here's a good suggestion for teaching your teen how to behave on a date: Grab a couple of movies to see examples of a good date (Buddy in *Elf*) and a bad one (Gru in *Despicable Me 2*).

> In this bad date, Gru isn't being himself, he's wearing a wig! His date is constantly talking about herself, insulting him, and embarrassing him. She's also very negative. All things to avoid, of course!! (If you have access to the whole movie, you may want to rewind and watch a little more of the date.)
>
> Good Date Example: Your teenager doesn't need to learn to sing their true love to the whole world like Buddy, but Buddy the Elf is a great example of being happy and smiling the whole time on this date. He compliments his date and has a series of fun activities planned for the night. Even though he acts a little goofy, Jovi is a good sport and goes with it, even if it's not necessarily her idea of fun. They end up having a great time together![10]

Some Final Words

There's another factor that has changed the landscape of teens and dating. In past generations, there was an expectation and urgency for teens to start the search for a life mate and get married. In the 1970s, the average age for men's first marriages was about twenty-three, and about twenty-one for women. Now men are approaching thirty and women are over twenty-seven for first marriages.[11] Recognize that no matter how things were when you were dating, some teens feel no hurry for dating or other exclusive relationships.

An emerging issue that dominates teen relationships is the reality of consent. Although we alluded to it in the chapter on boundaries, more and more emphasis is placed on whether or not both participants of any physical relationship express vocally and specifically their permission to proceed at any point, from a physical brush across the shoulders all the way to intercourse (if it goes that far). In a #MeToo culture, no wonder young men are afraid to even look sexually insistent. For many with scholarships and jobs and reputations at risk, they may think it's safer to not have a physical relationship, or to wait for a partner to initiate and approve it, or pay for sex or porn. In their minds, dating may just not be worth the trouble.

EXPLORATION
WITH YOUR TEEN

1. Any discussion with your kid about dating and sex (and its blessing to a marriage) should also include the acknowledgment that a celibate single life is also not only acceptable to God, but He actually commanded it in certain circumstances.[12] And remember, our model and example, Jesus, stayed single because of some of the factors in those Scriptures.

2. Consider this quotation and discuss it with your teen: "Paul's rationale for sexual morality is that your body has the dignity of being a member of the body of Christ, the locus of his presence on earth. Paul then says something truly stunning: 'Your bodies are temples of the Holy Spirit' ([1 Corinthians 6] v.19). The temple

was sacred space, where people went to meet with God. Astonishingly, this passage is saying that your body is where people will meet God. And other people's bodies are where *you* will see God."[13] Ask your teen this: How can you look for and appreciate God's characteristics reflected in someone you date?

3. Ask questions of your teen that researchers are asking: Why do you think young adults spend a lot of time in groups and not dating as much as they did in times past? Is there anything you'd like to know about how to ask someone on a date? And what is a date, anyhow?

EIGHT

Sexual Abuse and Violence

In my practice as a counselor, I meet wonderful kids in horrible situations. They desperately need someone to listen without judgment, and to show them a clear path out of the situation. I've been privileged to counsel and help kids who've undergone three types of abuse—sexual abuse, incest, and rape—and offer their stories to you. But, of course, the best solution is prevention, and their stories can give insight on this.

Maria's Story: Sexual Abuse

When I first met Maria, I saw an attractive dark-haired young woman overcome by regret and grief. She was attending a college two thousand miles from her home because she felt she needed physical distance from a relationship in order to heal. What happened to her in high school had caused her to doubt her sexuality, her status with God (even though she's attended church faithfully her whole life), and her value as a friend.

The first two issues—her sexuality and her status with God—emerge in our conversation. She's kept a terrible secret for four years, trying not to hurt anyone involved. I see her pain as she explains how her mom became friends with Maria's eighth-grade softball coach, a woman named Jaclyn. Jaclyn's own mother was diagnosed with cancer, and Maria's mom became the primary emotional support for the coach.

Maria mirrored her mother's compassion and began to send cards and Bible verses to her coach to encourage her. Maria's whole family was devastated when Jaclyn's mom succumbed to her illness. Jaclyn became even closer to Maria after that, confiding her grief and other private thoughts to Maria.

Though she was initially a bit uncomfortable with Maria having a peer relationship with the coach, Maria's mom reasoned that since this was happening at a Christian school, the relationship might be beneficial to both and would naturally taper off.

Except it didn't.

When Jaclyn accepted a last-minute invitation to a women's retreat at a Christian camp in the mountains, she asked Maria to ride with her to help navigate. When they arrived, there weren't enough rooms, but Maria was happy to share her room with her beloved coach. They talked into the night about how Jaclyn continued to miss her mom. Maria felt she was truly serving a need for Jaclyn.

In the middle of the night, Maria was awakened by Jaclyn's hand caressing her breast.

"I thought she must be doing it in her sleep, like dreaming," Maria tells me. "So I just stayed still until it was over." And then the next morning, Jaclyn acted as if she were unaware of what had happened. But it happened again the next night. This was the beginning of an increasingly intense four-year sexual relationship that Maria hated but felt powerless to stop. Maria wanted to tell her mom, but what would her mother think about

Jaclyn? Would Jaclyn get in trouble? Her mom might not let her see Jaclyn anymore, and Jaclyn told Maria all the time that she needed her help to cope with her mother's death.

The only escape Maria found was going far, far away to college. But even now, eighteen months after breaking off the relationship with Jaclyn, she sits before me in my office and still wonders if she has abandoned a friend who needed her. She can't cover all the bases in her life and feel good about her sexuality. How can you be a good Christian with a situation like this?

It's true that we should feel guilt when we've done something wrong—appropriate guilt is a signal from the Holy Spirit that leads us to recognize wrongdoing, to repent, to learn from mistakes, to seek forgiveness from God and move forward. But guilt is a weapon used by sexual predators: In Maria's case, if Jaclyn hadn't kept insisting that she couldn't function without Maria's support with her grief, the abuse would never have continued.

Maria's mom had the best of intentions. Maria's reaching out to her coach was commendable and loving. But the coach was an adult and should have sought emotional support from adults, not a teenager.

Parents sometimes don't realize how important it is to keep a child from becoming an emotional support for an adult in authority over him or her. As a parent, you have to be strong-minded about any person who has access to your child. Your teen doesn't have the life experience to evaluate the influence of others as you do. You have to watch out for those who would take advantage of their trust. It's an old, old story: Ezekiel 34:2–4 gives an unforgettable picture of unscrupulous people in authority over the vulnerable and compares them to shepherds who care only for themselves and take advantage of others.[1]

Maria was torn between her good motives—her desire to protect the emotional stability and reputation of Jaclyn—and the knowledge that the relationship was eating away at her own soul. Until she understood she had lost control of what was happening, she never realized how such abuse could make the abuser even bolder in taking advantage of others.

Maria is one of 1.3 million children who have been sexually abused by someone they trusted and admired. If Maria's mom had known what to look for, she might have recognized the symptoms of abuse. But that can be difficult. If teens have been repeatedly sexually abused since childhood, there may not be noticeable "red flag" changes in their behavior during adolescence. However, if an abusive sexual relationship begins during adolescence, marked changes in a teen's behavior can be a warning sign.

Unfortunately, different teens exhibit different symptoms when they are sexually abused. In addition, some of these same symptoms may indicate other problematic issues in teens' lives. The emergence of several of these symptoms, particularly sexual symptoms, should raise concerns.

TYPES OF SYMPTOMS	SYMPTOMS OF SEXUAL ABUSE
Physical Symptoms	Insomnia, headaches, stomachaches, vomiting, nausea, pregnancy, or sexually transmitted diseases
Sexual Symptoms	Wearing seductive clothing, engaging in seductive posturing, removing clothing in inappropriate situations, openly asking for sex, having sex with multiple partners, engaging in prostitution or sexually aggressive behaviors, masturbating frequently or in public, or developing an aversion to anything sexual
Emotional Symptoms	Depression, anger, anxiety, sudden mood changes, crying easily or frequently, being irritable, or making negative statements about one's self

TYPES OF SYMPTOMS	SYMPTOMS OF SEXUAL ABUSE
Behavioral Symptoms	Changes in sleeping or eating habits, poor hygiene, lack of concern about appearance, wearing loose-fitting clothing, changes in school grades or performance in class, withdrawal from family or friends, refusing to comply with adult requests, or being overly compliant with adult requests
Delinquent Symptoms	Drug or alcohol use, running away, truancy, aggressiveness, or bullying

Why Teens Don't Report

Even though teens may recognize that sexual interactions with adults are wrong, they frequently do not report inappropriate sexual contact with adults. Here are some reasons:

- Teens think no one will believe them. That's because sexual offenders often threaten teens and tell them no one will believe them. In some situations, the sexual offender is a highly respected member of the church community with more credibility than the child.

- Teens genuinely care about the sexual perpetrator and don't want the perpetrator punished. Remember, as in Maria's case, the sexual offender may be a close family friend who has already established an emotional relationship with the teen before engaging in sexual activity.

- Teens feel tremendous guilt about the sexual behavior and don't want other people to know about it. A teen may feel soiled physically, emotionally, or spiritually by having sexual contact with an adult. As a result, teens have a sense of unworthiness and blame themselves for the sexual contact.

- Our society makes a big deal about not giving consent to sexual acts. But teens may mistakenly believe that because they didn't (or weren't able to) fight off a perpetrator, they have consented. Teens cannot EVER consent to having sex with an adult.

- Teens may see the sexual relationship with the adult as romantic and want the sexual contact to continue. But despite the teen's feelings about the relationship, this much is true: *The adult is always at fault, both legally and morally, for engaging in a sexual relationship with a minor. Even if a teen initiates some sexual behavior, it is the adult's responsibility to stop any sexual behavior immediately.*

- Teens sometimes don't know where to get help and don't know who they can trust. Similarly, they don't know if adults are capable of dealing with the disclosure.

- Teens are often afraid of how their parents will react, so they may ease into introducing the subject, or if they don't know if an adult will be capable of helping them deal with sexual abuse, they may drop hints about the perpetrator, or they may try to "get caught."

Emma's Story: Incest

From the time Emma first picked out a tune on a toy piano, her parents, Natalie and Steve, could tell this child had extraordinary talent. They paid for piano lessons, and she excelled at them.

The interest in music came from Steve's side of the family. Steve's younger brother, Trent, worked as a professional musician. Steve thought Trent was maturing when he enrolled in college for a music degree and began teaching choir once he graduated.

When Natalie's daughter, Emma, expressed interest in stringed instruments, Trent offered to give her lessons. Natalie and Steve were proud of her progress and her increasing skill at guitar and operating a sound board as Trent taught her.

"But then I found a pregnancy test—negative—in Emma's bathroom trash can," Natalie tells me.

I see her face reflecting an inner whirlwind of emotions, and I wait until she can regain her composure.

"She was crying as she saw it in my hand and of course I was just stunned. I didn't even know she had a boyfriend."

I lean back. "So not being pregnant—that was good news, right?"

The emotion I see now is clearly anger.

"At first she couldn't even talk. She just sobbed and sobbed. Finally, she was able to tell me that she'd done the test and it was negative. But—she had an STD. I just held her close and tried to comfort her. She trembled all over and I know she needed my support right then more than I needed details."

Wise mom, I thought. As Natalie continues, she describes how it finally came out that Trent had forced Emma into sexual acts to "pay" for her music lessons. And like many teens, she mistakenly believed a relationship with someone older was a sign of her maturity. Instead, it highlighted her vulnerability.

"I wanted to tear his head off," Natalie says. "But instead I called my husband, Steve, to come home, and then we contacted a friend who is in law enforcement. The police took it from there. And that monster will never hurt Emma or any other kid again."

Through their experiences with Emma, Steve and Natalie learned the following:

- When a teen tells you of any kind of abuse, *don't promise confidentiality*. That's a promise you can't afford to keep under any circumstances. If a teen tells you that he or she is engaged in a sexual relationship with an adult, you will have to report the situation to authorities.

- *Believe the story.* As a general rule, teens do not make up stories about being sexually abused. You need to assume the story is true. You don't have the skills to determine if a teen is making up an accusation.

- *Assure teens it is not their fault.* An adult is always responsible for initiating a sexual relationship with a teen. Even if a teen tries to initiate a sexual relationship with an adult, it is the adult's job to maintain an appropriate physical and sexual relationship with a teen.

- *Develop a safety plan.* Immediately strategize how to keep the teen away from the perpetrator. If the perpetrator is a family member, you may need to cut off all contact with the perpetrator and supervise contact with any family members who do not believe your child.

- *Notify authorities.* In most states, if the teen is under seventeen years of age, you are legally required to report any suspected abuse to the police or a child protection agency. Don't let a family member persuade you to ignore the situation or not report the situation. If an adult has abused your child, he or she will abuse other children.

- *Obtain medical help.* If a sexual assault has just occurred, you need to take the teen to a rape crisis center or emergency room for medical care. Do not allow a teen to shower or clean up after an assault. Law enforcement will need to examine your teen for forensic evidence. The forensic nurses I have worked with have been compassionate and kind in their work with children and teens.

- If a teen who is not your child tells you about being sexually assaulted, *you are required to report the assault* to law enforcement and allow the child or law enforcement to let their parents know.

The anger and offense Natalie felt are good things. We as Christians sometimes think about patience and long-suffering as (sometimes unattainable) ideals in any situation. But Jesus showed white-knuckle anger when He talked about situations like Emma's. He said, "Whoever causes one of these little ones who believe in me to sin, it would be better for him to have a great millstone fastened around his neck and to be drowned in the depth of the sea" (Matthew 18:6 ESV). You see, as we illustrated in our previous book, *How to Protect Your Child from Predators*, Jesus was absolutely infuriated with anyone who took a child's innocence. He is a warrior, and you also should be a warrior in protecting your teen.

Julie's Story: Date Rape

Julie was thrilled when Ken, who was a grade ahead of her, invited her to a party at his parents' house. He was a leader in the church youth group, and his parents were supervising the party, so Julie's parents shared in her excitement at the invitation. When they got there, Ken's attentiveness and his arm around her shoulder made her feel special. He laughed at her jokes and got her a soda and snacks. With his parents and so many other kids so close by in the house and out on the patio, she wasn't a bit uncomfortable when he asked if she'd like to see his room. He opened the door for her and she walked in, still flattered by his gentlemanly treatment.

"But as soon as that door closed behind me, it's like he became a different person," Julie tells me. "He started kissing me, and it got more—" she searches for a word—"forceful.

And I tried to back away from him, but he was pushing me toward the bed."

She is crying now and goes on to describe how Ken pinned her to the bed, put a forearm across her throat, and began ripping off her panties and unzipping his jeans.

"I couldn't breathe," Julie says. "He was on top of me, and then . . . inside me, and there was nothing I could do. I was afraid I was going to die."

I nod with sympathy.

"And just as quick as he finished, he let me go and told me to hurry up, get myself cleaned up. I was just lying there, shaking and crying. So he zipped his pants and tucked in his shirt and leaned over and said things to me."

"What did he say?" I wait for her to stop crying.

"He said not to tell anyone, that nobody would believe me if I did. And that I'd wanted it just like he did, and I was a slut and everyone would know it if I told. Then he told me to smile and act happy. And when we walked back into the living room, I guess nobody even noticed we'd been gone. And he just acted like nothing at all had happened."

Julie is representative of teens who will experience date rape.

- Of sexual abuse cases reported to law enforcement, 93 percent of juvenile victims knew the perpetrator.[2]
- The younger a female is, the more likely it is that she was forced to have sex.[3]

In Julie's case, she didn't immediately tell anyone about the rape because Ken convinced her she was to blame. However, she eventually told a friend in her youth group about the incident during a week at church camp. Julie's friend talked with a youth worker, and the truth of the story emerged. With counseling and the support of her family, Julie is able to move past this incident.

EXPLORATION
WITH YOUR TEEN

Just as we role-play with younger kids about what to do when approached by a stranger, we can role-play with teens to help them anticipate situations. For instance, we can remind them how sometimes people will try to lure kids by asking for help finding a lost puppy. Just as adults don't need little kids' help finding a pet, they similarly don't need the companionship and time alone with a teenager.

In our book *Protecting Your Child from Predators: How to Recognize and Respond to Sexual Danger*, I offer the following strategies and urge you to implement these with your teen. Role-play situations with your teen ahead of time with a light touch in the conversations. Make a chart for yourself in a journal that has a calendar. For each discussion topic below, choose a calendar date by which you'll initiate a conversation about the topic.

- Discuss with your teen what sexual and emotional limits are healthy in a relationship and how to tell other people about those limits. Write on your chart the date you plan to do this.

- If someone has violated the emotional or sexual limits your teen sets, your teenager should recognize that it is dangerous and speak up immediately. Assure your child that you will always operate on the assumption that they are not at fault, and you'll take protective action immediately. Write on your chart the date you plan to make sure your child knows you will welcome any such report and will not blame them.

- Let your teen know that they have the right to change their mind and say no, or that they can agree to kissing without agreeing to more sexual behaviors. Write on your chart the date you plan to discuss this.

- Teach your teen safety skills for group gatherings. Teach them to pour their own beverage and keep it in their sight. Help them to recognize how easily someone can put drugs or alcohol in their beverages. Likewise, teach your teenagers to be aware of where they are hanging out and to avoid places that keep them isolated from others. Teens may feel like they can take care of themselves, but they don't have the life experiences to recognize when they are in danger. Write on your chart the date you plan to discuss group safety with your child.

- Help your teens learn to trust their instincts regarding danger. The Holy Spirit is a protector too. If they feel that a person or situation is not safe, they should leave immediately. Write on your chart the date you'll discuss this. Here are some Scriptures to show the protectiveness of God's Spirit in the lives of His people:

  - **Psalm 46:1** ESV—"God is our refuge and strength, a very present help in trouble."

  - **1 Corinthians 2:12** ESV—"Now we have received not the spirit of the world, but the Spirit who is from God, that we might understand the things freely given us by God."

  - **Psalm 138:7** ESV —"Though I walk in the midst of trouble, you preserve my life; you stretch out your hand against the wrath of my enemies, and your right hand delivers me."

  - **John 16:13** ESV—"When the Spirit of truth comes, he will guide you into all the truth, for he will not speak on his own authority, but whatever he hears he will speak, and he will declare to you the things that are to come."

- Help your teens recognize that they need a backup plan no matter where they go. This plan should include telling someone they trust where they are going. They should always have a person to call who will come immediately to get them. Agree on an "alert" word the teen can use in an unsafe situation that will bring help immediately and/or give them an out to get away. Discuss an alert word and make sure you and your teen have the word recorded somewhere on your phones. Remind them often of the alert word.

NINE

Social Media and Technology

They met at a regional youth conference and exchanged contact information. At first, it was just friend stuff—texting funny memes and video chatting. Heather has a natural, dry sense of humor, and she liked that in her new friend Brandon, who got her inside jokes from movies they both liked. They soon began talking about creating a funny TikTok video—a popular teen social media site for short, creative comedy sketches. No doubt about it, Heather and Brandon had a connection. But they lived miles away from each other, didn't drive, went to different schools, and sometimes, as Brandon told her, it didn't seem like enough. And they both knew they liked each other as more than friends now.

Heather's parents understood the urgencies of teen romances but were wisely protective of their sixteen-year-old daughter. When they turned down the idea of her getting together with Brandon to create a video, Heather was disappointed. Then Brandon sent messages to Heather about how stupid her parents were. He missed her, he said, and asked her to at least send some pictures.

He told her how pretty she was in her first set of pictures. But they were getting so close, couldn't she send some that are a little more personal? She didn't want to lose her first boyfriend. What could it hurt?

First cleavage. Then underwear. It felt daring and so adult.

She stopped to think about what the Bible said, but only for a moment. Nope, it said nothing. This wasn't sex, it was just communication. And besides, it never would have come to this if her parents had just let them see each other, make the video.

Then, because he said he needed them, she sent the nude photos.

Finally, another youth conference rolled around and Brandon went. He seemed bored and nervous, though, and texted her to meet him in an empty classroom. Once they entered the classroom, Brandon immediately began kissing Heather and trying to put his hands under her shirt. She shoved him away and told him to stop.

He gave her a long look, then scrolled over to the nude pictures of Heather stored on his phone.

"If you make me stop, I'll share these pictures with my friends. It's up to you. They like sharing pictures too. Who knows where they might go. Your brother might even see them."

Heather's flash of anger was followed by fear and shame. Those pictures were meant for his eyes only. But other people! Her parents would kill her if they knew she had sent Brandon nude pictures.

What happened later in the classroom, Heather tells me, was the lesser of two evils. She couldn't imagine those pictures becoming public. She, like many other youth of today, had learned what sextortion is, a form of blackmail in which sexual information or images are used to extort sexual favors. It all started with sexting—the sending, receiving, or forwarding of sexually explicit messages, photographs, or images via technology.

Remember the sin template of Adam and Eve we talked about in chapter 2? It starts with questioning in a new situation, and wondering if maybe God didn't address this, so it would be all right. Then it involves planning and reasoning and the senses and imagination. In that classroom, it ended with consequences and shame and sorrow. Just as it did in the garden of Eden.

Sexting

In sexting, Heather and Brandon were taking part in a fairly common teen practice, as 22 percent of teen girls report that they have sent or posted nude or semi-nude photos or videos of themselves, while 18 percent of same-age boys have, and 39 percent of teens say they have sent sexually suggestive messages via text, email, or instant messaging.[1] In addition, 71 percent of teen girls and 67 percent of teen boys "who have sent or posted sexually suggestive content say they have sent/posted this content to a boyfriend/girlfriend."[2] Nearly 75 percent of teens recognize that sending suggestive content "can have serious negative consequences,"[3] and 44 percent of teens say "it is common for sexually suggestive text messages to get shared with people other than the intended recipient."[4]

Like Heather, nearly four in ten teens believe that "exchanging sexually suggestive content makes dating or hooking up with others more likely."[5] While 51 percent of teen girls cite pressure from a male as a reason that girls send sexy messages or images, only 18 percent of teen boys say pressure from females is a reason.[6]

Sexting Guidelines

The ideal time to talk to your kids about sexting is before they are involved in a sexting incident. Damage control after an incident is nearly impossible, because once an image is sent it can never be retrieved. Even if all technology on the earth ceased tomorrow, a printout of a picture can still exist in the hands of a complete stranger.

Your teen may even know a horror story about sexting from friends at school. Empathy is a powerful tool. Ask your teen to think about how they would feel about kids at school and church seeing the images they send. Because of the ease of and lack of control over technology, once they send an image, they have in essence given blanket permission for anyone in the world to view it, distribute it, even sell it.

Yes, you can acknowledge that there's great pressure for a teen to sext another teen. Many teens think—and rightly so—that they'll be rejected by someone they really want a relationship with if they refuse. But reason with them: If a revealing picture is going to be a make-it-or-break-it feature of your relationship, is that person really worth pursuing? Is the humiliation of having revealing photos distributed to strangers really easier to contemplate than figuring out some strategies to not send them in the first place?

Accountability is one strategy. Tell your teen you know about sexting and how commonplace it is. Discuss the dangers of it. Then ask them to promise never, ever to send another suggestive text, image, or video. Ever. To stop it in its tracks.

Strategy two: Remind your teen that you own their cell phone and must have the passwords to the phone and all its apps. Require that all electronic devices be docked and charged in the kitchen each night. (Actually, you should be doing that already.)

Here's another strategy: They may not be able to stop sexting worldwide, but your teen can press the delete button when they receive one. Imagine the power of slaying just one dragon at a time! And if they have questions about an image or video, you commit to them that you will not judge them for bringing it to you.

Internet Predators

Thirteen-year-old Christina lives with her aunt and attends a private religious school in a small town. Everybody loves this girl—she is involved in cheerleading, is a good student, and is an altar girl at church. She is spirited and outgoing with her friends and makes everyone, including adults, laugh at her wry humor.

She's adept with technology too. Nobody in that town knows the Christina who has her own website and a dozen provocative screen names in chat rooms, where she is known for her sexual vocabulary and wit. Christina loves the attention she gets online and even agrees to meet men face-to-face.

The night Christina's aunt dropped her off at the mall "to meet some friends," her aunt didn't know that the man Christina met up with was someone she'd met before, for sex. Everything had gone smoothly last time.

Christina never returned home to her pom-poms and computer. Police eventually found her body and determined that she was strangled by the man she met to have sex.

For Christina, for you, for your teen, for everyone, the internet is a giant bay window into your home. If you leave the lights on at night and the curtains open, someone will look. Someone will strategize about how to get in. If they want your kid, they may pretend to be a kid. Sexual predators are incredibly patient. They go slowly. They will take notes on what they observe and ask all the best questions to get more information. Soon they don't have to just look in the window. They'll find out how to get in the door. Your teens, like Christina, may willingly give them keys, passwords, family secrets, their bra sizes, and their sexual selves.

The image of a bay window can illustrate the real access to your home. If a predator can't persuade a teen to meet with him as did Christina, he will bide his time. This is a slow process, a long haul with a big payoff, and he's willing to take months to do it. Maybe he will find out your home address. Most preda-tors attempting to lure minors into sex through digital com-munication are using social media sites, chat features of video games, and apps.[7] Law enforcement officials estimate that more than 50,000 sexual predators are online at any given moment.[8] In a very literal sense, sexual predation never sleeps, its wide-open eyes constantly roaming the bay windows of teens. Many are quite experienced: Approximately 70 percent of all sex of-fenders released from prison will offend again.[9]

Don't fool yourself that this isn't happening all around you: Almost 70 percent of teens "regularly receive online commu-nications from strangers" and don't tell their parents; one in five teen internet users has experienced unwanted sexual solici-tation, and about 89 percent of sexual solicitation of youths happens in chat rooms or through messaging.[10]

If someone you did not know walked up to you on the street and complimented you on what you were wearing, you would probably thank them and walk away. If the same stranger saw you the next day and offered a different compliment, you might think it was a little odd. If the same person continued to stop you on the street to offer compliments, you probably would feel threatened and try to avoid him or her. We all know about stranger danger, right?

Yet when something similar happens through social media, we don't seem to recognize that it is unusual and suspect. Be-cause the conversation is online and the other person is anony-mous, we tend to think the conversation is entirely harmless and simply complimentary. Amazing how a computer screen can empower us to feel so secure when we aren't secure at all.

With teens, everyday conversations on social media channels such as Twitter or Snapchat quickly transition to private direct messaging and sharing of personal information. This has be-come a norm. Teens can't imagine a world without technology. The stranger giving compliments on the street would need to go to a lot of trouble to disguise himself for each meeting. On the internet, he just has to change his name and he can find out something new every time.

Social Media

There has been a 300 percent increase in the number of sexual assault cases related to social media sites, and 29 percent of "internet sex crime relationships were initiated on a social media site."[11] In 26 percent of online sex crimes against minors, offenders disseminated information and/or images of the victim through the victim's social media sites.[12]

Meeting people online is risky at any age, but it is especially so for teenagers because they don't have the life experience to recognize when they are being deceived or manipulated. Here are some of the factors:

- *Anonymity*. Part of the allure of initiating relationships in chat rooms and through instant messenger technology is the ability to be anonymous. But it comes with a price: Inhibitions fall when someone is wearing a virtual mask. He or she is much more willing to engage in inappropriate or risky behaviors, and it gives the illusion of invisibility: 39 percent of teens "think their online activity is private from everyone, including parents."[13]

- *Access*. The internet has millions of bay windows open to kids. And kids don't have the life experience to keep them from trusting likeable strangers who seem "too far away" to do them any real harm. So if a predator says he's a struggling teenage rock musician in London, what's the problem in letting him know your address?

- *Acceptance*. Using the internet as a way to communicate and establish relationships is part of business, part of church life, part of our social fabric. Parents and other adults may not view the internet as threatening because it's so useful, so essential. They may not recognize that people accessing teens on the internet may present a physical or sexual threat to a teen.

- *Different rules.* Through the internet, teens frequently share personal information and develop relationships with anonymous individuals. Remarkably, 55 percent of teens have given out personal information, including photos and physical descriptions, to someone they don't know.[14] Parents who wouldn't dream of allowing teens to engage in the same level of disclosure and emotional intimacy in a personal face-to-face relationship without some level of screening and supervision fire up the router and hope for the best.

Warning Signs

What should alert you to the likelihood that your teen is involved in sexting or sexual behavior on social media? Each of the following can be symptomatic of many things, but a combination of them should get your attention.

- Your teen is secretive about online activities and changes screens or turns off device screens when an adult comes into the room.
- They become very possessive of their devices.
- The teen is defensive, often angry or crying, when you question cell phone or computer use.
- The teen deletes call histories, texts, and internet history.
- A teen's "real life" circle of friends changes or seems to be much less important than before.

- A teen's grades change.
- He or she seems obsessed with their phone or other internet-connected device and becomes agitated when online access isn't available.
- He or she gets unexplained telephone calls, gifts, or packages.

Internet Safety

You have to take charge here.

- *Monitor internet access.* With so many digital devices available, you have to be "eyes on" your teen's devices. Use monitoring software to see what teens are doing online. Their privacy? This is their safety we're talking about.
- *Be proactive.* They are already one step ahead of you, as 67 percent of teenagers say they know how to hide what they do online from their parents, and 43 percent say "they would change their online behavior if they knew their parents were watching them."[15]
- *Use a filter.* Install one on computers and routers to prevent teens from accessing websites that have pornographic material or other objectionable content.
- *Protect everyone's identity.* Have a family meeting and write out rules: Don't give out your name, your address, or other personal information on the internet—or any such information about any family member or friend. For teens, don't identify where you go to high school, where you work, or where you go to church. Similarly, don't give out information about your gender or age.
- *Strangers not allowed.* Interact online only with people you know. Don't use the internet to develop

relationships with strangers. For teens, the dangers far outweigh the benefits because teens don't have the skills to determine who is appropriate and inappropriate on the internet.

- *Do some research.* Use up-to-date sources for your information, especially regarding apps—new ones come out all the time. In our book *Protecting Your Child from Predators*, I give solid, doable strategies concerning social media that are too numerous to list here. But think of updating your knowledge and strategies the same way you make a grocery list: You have to do it regularly. You can't afford to run out of food or tactics. Your teens are very, very smart. And the predators and social engineers of this dark world are even smarter.

Final Words

You may have noticed that the language of this chapter is more combative than it is in others. In general, when people talk about teens and sex, we operate on the assumption that guys and girls alike get into trouble with hormonal urges and just plain teenage ignorance of the real world. We may even take into consideration their developing brains. Like God the Parent who looks at us, we look with compassion on the hard teenage years.

> As a father has compassion on his children,
>   so the LORD has compassion on those who fear him;
> for he knows how we are formed,
>   he remembers that we are dust.
> The life of mortals is like grass,
>   they flourish like a flower of the field;
> the wind blows over it and it is gone,
>   and its place remembers it no more.
>
> Psalm 103:13–16

We know that this time of their life is only temporary, and we want to be merciful to them and help them achieve their best, and for all of us to survive it together.

The kids aren't the enemy. Your teens are the prey. There are highly financed and highly motivated people who want to sexualize your kids.

They are the enemy, and you must not tolerate them.

EXPLORATION
WITH YOUR TEEN

1. Ask your teens if they know someone who's gotten in trouble with sexting. Don't ask for names, just for the scenario. Then discuss how that situation could have been avoided. Create a pie chart on a piece of paper showing the relative value of the potential dating situation compared with the potential for ongoing hurt and shame if pictures become public.

2. Read together with your teen the following in Colossians 3:2–6:

> Set your minds on things above, not on earthly things. For you died, and your life is now hidden with Christ in God. When Christ, who is your life, appears, then you also will appear with him in glory. Put to death, therefore, whatever belongs to your earthly nature: sexual immorality, impurity, lust, evil desires and greed, which is idolatry. Because of these, the wrath of God is coming.

- Ask your teen: What would help you to set your mind above, not on earthly things? You may want to brainstorm about replacing a social media app with a journaling app, for instance.

- Or your teen might choose a prayer partner and commit to a certain time each day to compose a prayer on behalf of the friend and text it to the friend.
- You might study the concept of fasting and discuss with your teen a "tech fast" for a certain period of a day, or a longer length of time of not using a phone or other electronic form of communication. Show fellowship with your teen by doing the same.

TEN

This Is Your Teen's Brain on Porn

Tim Challies, a popular Canadian blogger and author, has spoken on four continents to tens of thousands of Christians. "Everywhere I go, I lay down the same challenge," Challies says. "If you're male between the ages of eighteen and twenty-five and you have never once gone looking for pornography online, just come and talk to me afterwards. I'd love to hear about it. . . . Not one has ever come up to me and said, 'Yes, that's me.'"[1]

Not one.

Sad Facts

Unfortunately, from my own case files, I can't offer a different view. Are you shocked by this story? In fact, only 12 percent of parents know their teens are accessing pornography.[2]

About 70 percent of children ages eight to eighteen are exposed to porn accidentally, many times quite innocently as they do internet research for homework assignments.[3] (I talked at length about this in *Protecting Your Child from Predators* in "The Wikipedia Ambush" chapter.) Once exposed, most teens go on to become regular consumers of pornography. Would it surprise you to know that the largest group of internet porn consumers are teens ages twelve to seventeen?[4] That 90 percent of children ages eight to sixteen have seen online porn?[5]

They're no longer just stumbling across it, as "32% of teens admit to intentionally accessing nude or pornographic content online. Of these, 43% do so on a weekly basis."[6]

One of the strongest motivations I can give parents for having early, regular talks about sex with their teens is that teens' sex education will come from porn if parents don't do the teaching. Sixty percent of teens said they watch porn in order to learn more about sex and learn about gaps in their sexual education (even though 75 percent admitted porn creates unrealistic expectations).[7]

You see, even teens realize this is a problem. Eight out of ten eighteen-year-olds think it is too easy for young people to accidentally see pornography online.[8]

What Is Porn?

Pornographic materials include

- internet websites,
- sexting,
- virtual reality games,
- telephone sex lines,
- pornographic magazines and books,
- peep shows,
- adult cable programming, and
- live sex acts and strip clubs.

Even the language we use about porn has changed in recent years. In the past, the static forms of porn usually available to teens—so called "girlie magazines," movies, or strip clubs, for instance—were something you "looked at" or "watched." Today, porn can be something you *experience* through emerging forms such as virtual reality in which interaction is possible.

What Does Pornography Depict?

- Nudity
- Child pornography
- Heterosexual activities
- Incest pornography
- Homosexual activities
- Sex with animals
- Violent sexual activities
- Sexual activities intended to humiliate or torture
- Group sex

This Is Your Brain on Porn

Before we discuss the moral implications of pornography, let's look at the physical effects.

Internet pornography damages the brains of children of all ages: It literally shrinks the amount of gray matter in their brains as hours of reported pornography use increase. The brain begins to lose the ability to function properly.[9] Teens are also at a great risk of developing a pornography addiction as their brains are still developing[10] (although parents might ruefully speculate that something about the teenage years causes brains to stop developing for a few years anyhow).

This addiction is like all other addictions. Researchers believe that pornography's intense stimulation of the brain brings about significant changes to the brain similar to those of drug addiction.[11] Why? Our brains react to pornography the same way an alcoholic might react to seeing a drink advertisement.[12]

And as in other addictions, a porn addict needs bigger "highs," increasing setpoints for satisfaction. "Like other addictive triggers, pornography floods the brain with dopamine. That rush of brain chemicals, when it happens repeatedly, rewires the brain's reward pathway and can become a default setting."[13] There's a reason we call addictions "habits."

Another way to visualize the plasticity of neurons in the brain, and the way they can figuratively fuse together, is the so-called Hebbian theory, which states that brain cells that fire together, wire together. In the words of brain scientist Dr. Janet Zadina, "What you pay attention to changes the brain in that direction."[14]

Upping the Ante

It's not bad enough that brains shrink and become rewired; it gets worse. Exposure to pornography between ages nine and thirteen is linked to high-risk behaviors.[15] Teens who view pornography

- have stronger gender stereotypes about sexual behavior,
- become sexually active at a younger age,
- engage in more casual sexual behavior, and
- have increased sexual aggression.[16]

How does this play out in behavior? Viewing porn traps teens in a downward spiral. Of the 97 percent of teen males who viewed pornography, 23 percent said they tried to stop watching pornography but couldn't quit, and 13 percent reported they watched more and more violent and deviant types of pornography.[17] The ante keeps going up and up.

Not Just Guys

As you read those sobering statistics, your mind might be producing a mental image of a young man sitting in front of a screen. But an online survey revealed that 80 percent of females between the ages of sixteen and twenty have watched pornography. Of those females watching pornography, 8 percent reported that they could not quit watching it, and 10 percent stated that they (like their male counterparts) were watching more violent and deviant types of pornography.[18]

There are things the mind was never intended to contemplate. Even God has limits on what He thinks—He said in the book of Jeremiah that child sacrifice was not something He authorized, "nor did it enter my mind."[19] And yet detestable practices equally outside the contemplation of the infinite mind of God are things our youth are mentally engaging with daily.

By the time students attend college, 83 percent of males and 57 percent of females have seen group sex online; similarly, 69 percent of males and 55 percent of females have seen same-sex intercourse online.[20]

It gets worse.

Sexual bondage? Thirty-nine percent of males and 23 percent of college-age females have seen it online.[21]

Bestiality (as in humans having sex with animals)? Almost a third of males and a fifth of females in college have viewed that online.[22]

Who Produces This Stuff?

If your mental image of people who produce porn is that of seedy old men with cameras on a dingy movie set, revise that.

Teens also produce pornography. When teens produce pornography, usually on a webcam, more than 93 percent of the images feature young girls. Much of it is quite informal, almost casual. Almost half (46 percent) of teenagers say "sending sexual or naked photos or videos is part of everyday life for teenagers nowadays."[23]

Another moral issue sometimes overlooked is the devastating sex trafficking trade and the enslavement of innocent children and other God-created human souls to feed these addictions. If teens cannot be moved in any other way to examine the cost of pornography to themselves and their friends, perhaps they can consider this.

Spiritual Cost

Ultimately, and most significantly, pornography creates a chasm between God and the teen. Brains can only handle so much, and when teens become focused on sexual pleasure, it will always take the focus off God's will for their lives.

Porn destroys intimacy in relationships. No real-life person can compete with a myriad of fantasy sexual partners. Porn necessitates emotional detachment and a focus on pleasure, to such an extent that any real person's quirks and personality actually become burdensome.[24] And remember from our discussion in the intimacy chapter: Our human relationships mirror and depict aspects of our relationship with God. It's no wonder that teens who are involved with pornography can become socially isolated, and thus unable to connect with God. Their porn-numbed brains won't let them.

It affects families when teens become disconnected, distracted, detached. Family unity becomes the victim of a sin in which it doesn't participate, the secondhand smoke of porn.

People use the image of a slippery slope to warn about everything from politics to environmentalism. Teens might argue that porn is an end in itself. But it's the very nature of sin to masquerade as the solution to a need that will be without consequences, with nothing ahead on a slippery slope. True, you can't get pregnant or an STD from looking at images. But freedom from those specific consequences is a trade-off for the enslavement of the mind. Then an eventual participation in the actions depicted doesn't seem like such a big deal.

Now that you know how porn ravages brains and souls, truly ask yourself this question: Have you turned a blind eye to signals that your teen might be engaging in porn, reasoning, as they do, that at least they're not pregnant, can't get an STD, and are not using drugs?

Dealing with Pornography

Statistically speaking, your teenage boy is almost certainly viewing porn, and it's likely that your teenage girl is too. What can you do?

- *Define right from wrong.* If teens don't believe that viewing pornography is wrong or won't admit they are viewing it, then any other efforts to help them will be wasted. Examine your own views first. Are you seeing porn as a consolation prize for them not engaging in more overt behaviors? Do you see it as an inevitable part of sowing wild oats that will be satisfied by marriage? Can you articulate to yourself exactly what makes porn wrong?
- *Know the truth.* Many people believe that strong emotions and desires will become worse when stifled or repressed. But porn is addictive, and addicts can't have just a few drugs or just one drink to get by. Since that is the case, strategize ways to cut addictive porn off as completely as you can.

- *Accountability*. Discuss with your teen the anecdote from Tim Challies earlier in this chapter, and accept without judgment that your teen has viewed pornography, even if accidentally or unwillingly in "drive-by porn." Your relaxed attitude about this fact will relieve your teen. Then tell them that you or another adult you both decide upon will help them avoid looking at pornography.

- *Clean it out*. Help your teen think of ways to avoid access to pornography at school, work, and home. In the past, that may have meant just throwing out print material and not having premium channels on your television. Now it means safeguards on your internet service and phone accounts. It also means making sure teens can't access any technology when they are alone, and devising strategies for what to do when confronted by it with others. Our book *Protecting Your Child from Predators* has a whole section of such strategies.

- *Replace one thing with another*. If porn wires your brain into mental slavery, create some new neural pathways with the memorization of Scripture. Neurologists would agree that powerful language changes the brain when it's memorized. Don't discount the enormous power of the words of God fixed firmly in your child's brain! Here's what 2 Corinthians 10:3–5 says: "For though we live in the world, we do not wage war as the world does. The weapons we fight with are not the weapons of the world. On the contrary, *they have divine power to demolish strongholds*. We demolish arguments and every pretension that sets itself up against the knowledge of God, and *we take captive every thought to make it obedient to Christ*" (emphasis added). Here are some other Scriptures that deal with this issue of the mind: Philippians 4:4–8; Ephesians chapter 4; James 3:13–18 and 1:13–15; Colossians 3:1–8.

- *Call them to higher things.* Discuss with your teen that rejecting porn is a righteous thing to do: Do they really want to keep on having their time and minds consumed with porn? Do they want their watching of porn to increase? Just as disciplining your body at the gym makes it measurably stronger, the discipline of thinking on godly things makes your mind and soul strong. It is intensely satisfying to realize you are conquering a sin. Measurable ways to see progress are in a gratitude journal or even a chart app on the phone to mark when you've rejected an opportunity to view porn.

- *Get away.* A good example of one strategy is that of handsome young Joseph in Genesis, whose boss's wife lured him into her bedroom. He just turned and ran away. That was the smartest, strongest thing he could do. The smart, strong thing may be for a teen to use a single finger to turn off an electronic device either in private or in a group.

- *Count the cost.* Since porn is such a pervasive part of teen culture, rejecting it will have social consequences. It will certainly happen in secular situations and is likely to happen even in the church youth group. What's the trade-off? Be prepared to discuss that.

- *Get a life.* Frequently, pornography occupies so much time that teens don't have hobbies and other interests to occupy them. Help your teens find hobbies and activities they enjoy, and spend time with them in those activities or hobbies. If pornography has been substituted for relationships, teens may feel lonely and isolated. Consequently, teens may need help developing the skills to establish relationships with peers. Think of this as an investment in their careers. They will need healthy relationships in their jobs.

- *Get over the guilt.* Once teens acknowledge that pornography is wrong, they may feel a great deal of guilt about their behavior. Remind them that God loves them even if they don't believe they are worthy of His love. He loves them even when they sin.
- *Patience, please.* Teach teens to be patient with their setbacks. It took time for them to develop an interest in pornography, and it will take time to overcome it.

In Over Your Head

Your teen's porn addiction may be beyond your help. If the answer to any of the following questions is yes, your teen may need professional help.

- Has the teen tried to quit viewing pornography and failed?
- Is the teen continuing to increase the amount of time spent watching pornography?
- Is the teen viewing pornography on a regular basis for several hours a week?
- Is viewing pornographic material continuing to increase the frequency of masturbation?
- Is the teen watching other people undress or engage in sexual activities online?
- Is the teen fantasizing about rape or other violent sexual behaviors?
- Is the teen videotaping himself having sex with other people?

- Is the teen videotaping peers having sex?
- Is the teen involved in other inappropriate sexual behaviors?

Final Words

Porn is a big, big deal. It enslaves the brain in a physical sense, and it literally enslaves many in the sex trade. It is hardly a victimless crime against souls. Ephesians 4 is a blockbuster chapter, and verse 19 speaks of people who, "having lost all sensitivity . . . have given themselves over to sensuality so as to indulge in every kind of impurity, with a continual lust for more" (NIV1984).

Futile thinking. Darkened understanding. Hardened hearts. Separation from God. The whole chapter deals with the kinds of sins that "give the devil a foothold" (v. 27).

But then Paul tells of the ultimate victim of sins like porn. We all know what it means to lose someone precious to us, to mourn for what once was and is no more. Teens feel grief intensely, and you can harness the deep feelings of that concept to convey the price tag of porn. Such sins break the heart of God and put Him into mourning when we "grieve the Holy Spirit of God" (v. 30).

EXPLORATION
WITH YOUR TEEN

1. Discuss with your teen: The Bible often talks about the flesh or fleshly nature and how it has to be brought under control by a believer. Paul said, for instance, that he disciplined his body to keep it under subjection (1 Corinthians 9:27). What is the difference between thinking your body is yours to use, even abuse, as you

please, and disciplining it for service to the Lord? How could you convey that to your teen?

2. Print out and then read aloud Ephesians chapter 4 with your teen, marking with one color the destructive behaviors there and then with another color the effects of those sins. Then discuss what it might mean to grieve the Holy Spirit.

3. Billy Graham once told the story of an Eskimo man who had two dogs—one white and one black—that he'd take into town for weekly dogfights. The man would pit the dogs against each other and take bets. Sometimes the black dog would win, sometimes the white, but the man placed bets and seemed to have an uncanny ability to predict which one would win. Finally, someone asked him how he knew. He said, "I starve one and feed the other. The one I feed always wins because he is stronger."[25] Discuss this story with your teen and strategize how to feed or starve the practice of engaging in pornography. They may want to start with baby steps. Support and cheer them on in this.

4. Choose several of the Scriptures on self-control mentioned in this chapter and challenge your teen and yourself to memorize them. Reward yourselves for your success with paintball, laser tag, an amusement park date, or another activity your teen enjoys.

ELEVEN

Disorienting Sexuality

Renee is a youth minister who has worked with teens for nearly five years. Single, with no children of her own, she pours herself into this calling and connects exceptionally well with teens. Even in talking about dating and sexuality, she is comfortable and sets a relaxed and welcoming tone in the youth group discussions and activities.

Renee is surprised when Suzie, one of the parents, stops her after an evening Bible study. After some small talk about upcoming events, Suzie fidgets in her chair. Renee suddenly feels panicked, worried that Suzie's daughter, Chloe, might be in some sort of trouble.

"I'm not here about Chloe, exactly," Suzie begins. "She's a good kid. . . ."

Renee nods enthusiastically. Chloe is a sweet-natured sixteen-year-old with a great sense of humor who isn't a leader but always participates and tries to include others.

"You know Chloe has been good friends with Ava Roberts since they started elementary school together."

Renee nods. Ava has been Chloe's guest at youth group activities for years.

"They're 'besties,' as they say. Ava has practically lived at our house for several years when Chloe isn't living at her house. They've been inseparable for years. But . . ."

Renee waits as the mom tries to collect herself.

"Recently, Chloe confided in me that Ava believes she is a lesbian. Or, at least, she wants to 'explore' being lesbian. Ava has been hanging out with different friends at school. These new friends are labeled as 'lesbian' by the other teens." Suzie makes quote mark motions in the air.

"I'm worried. Chloe says she isn't interested in Ava in a sexual way at all, but I'm not sure that Ava isn't interested in Chloe. Chloe is so naïve, I'm not sure she would recognize if Ava tried to shift the relationship in a sexual way. Even if that doesn't happen, I'm concerned that Chloe will be labeled as a lesbian by other kids, just because she is friends with Ava. Once she gets labeled as a lesbian, she will have to live with that reputation for a long time and will probably be harassed.

"What am I supposed to do? Do I continue to let Chloe and Ava hang out together? Do I need to restrict the time they spend together? I mean, I feel like things have changed."

"Right about that," Renee says. "All teens want to explore their place in the world, their identity. Whereas a generation ago we may have done it with hairstyles and clothing and music, today's kids push their boundaries in even more ways. Everybody tells them that their bodies are their personal property and that they can choose new identities and even behaviors based on what they want and feel."

"I know," Suzie says.

"Honestly, I don't know what to tell you to do right now. I need some time to think about the situation. Let's get together the day after tomorrow," Renee says. "I'll reach out to some other youth ministers I know, do some reading, get some ideas for you. And let's both pray a lot!"

As a youth worker, Renee knows our culture teaches teens that sexual orientation is a choice and that teens are mature enough to make the choice to be heterosexual, homosexual, or bisexual. She knows that Suzie and she will need to set some groundwork, to accurately define sexual orientation as a teen's emotional and physical arousal in response to people of the same or opposite sex. A *heterosexual* is primarily attracted to teens of the opposite sex, while *homosexual* describes a teen who is primarily attracted to teens of the same sex. If teens are attracted to individuals of the same sex and the opposite sex too, they are identified as *bisexual*.

Sexual attraction exists whether a teen is sexually active or not: A teen can identify as heterosexual, homosexual, or bisexual and yet not be engaging in a sexual relationship with a peer. Interestingly, many individuals may not solidify their sexual orientation until adulthood.

Renee also recognizes that some parents confuse sexual orientation with gender identity. While *sexual orientation* describes sexual attraction, *gender identity* describes a person's internal sense of being male or female. Although the overwhelming majority of people have a gender identity that matches their anatomy, there are people who believe their gender identity does not match their anatomy. (This chapter will deal with sexual orientation, and the next will deal with gender identity and the intersection of gender identity and sexual orientation.)

Recent research shows that in the United States, 85 percent of teens identify as heterosexual, 2 percent identify as gay or lesbian, 8 percent identify as bisexual, and 4 percent are not sure of their sexual identity. Interestingly, the same research found that 45 percent of students had had sexual contact with only the opposite sex, 1.6 percent had had sexual contact with only the same sex, 5.3 percent had had sexual contact with both sexes, and 48 percent had had no sexual contact.[1] Keep in mind that sexual contact does not always indicate identity in regard to sexual orientation. As this research demonstrates, we have more teens *identifying* as homosexual or bisexual than are actually *engaging in* homosexual or bisexual behavior.

Today's teens are saturated in social media that doesn't accurately reflect how much teens are engaging in sexual behavior. Media and music present homosexuality as an acceptable lifestyle, with homosexual acts and relationships depicted as normal and even healthy. And in their daily lives, gay and lesbian youth alliances are being formed in public schools to help teens explore their sexual identities and to affirm their sexual orientation. As a result, teens routinely encounter gay and lesbian peers holding hands in the school hallways or escorting each other to school proms.

While a limited number of teens will legitimately struggle with homosexual attraction, many more are just exploring sexual orientation. In fact, statistically speaking, it is much more likely that your teen's questions will be about the homosexual attitudes of their friends than about their own struggles with homosexual behavior.

As our teens develop their identities, we need to provide support and accurate information for them rather than myths about sexuality and minimization or rejection of their struggles. We want them to seek *us* out for support rather than turning to peers or strangers for support who may provide inaccurate information and detrimental avenues of coping with the stress of confusion.

In contrast to the messages presented in the media, teens may still see peers who are homosexual being taunted and ridiculed. While there are schools where teens identifying themselves as homosexual can attend a prom together, there are also schools where such teens are shunned by their peers. Teens may hear their Christian friends making jokes, callous remarks, and cruel comments about homosexuality. These mixed messages leave teens confused about homosexuality.

At-Risk Behaviors

Teens who identify as homosexual or bisexual face substantial cultural stressors. Research shows that lesbian, gay, and bisexual high school students are at substantial risk for mental health and health issues. For instance, teens who identify as homosexual or bisexual are at greater risk for thinking about suicide, planning for suicide, and attempting suicide than their heterosexual peers.[2] Here are other at-risk behaviors of homosexual and bisexual teens compared with heterosexual teens and teens who aren't sure of their sexual orientation:

Table 1: At-Risk Behavior[3]

	HETEROSEXUAL	HOMOSEXUAL/ BISEXUAL	UNSURE
1. Considered suicide	13.3%	47.7%	31.8%
2. Been electronically bullied	13.3%	27.1%	22.0%
3. Had safety concerns about school	6.1%	10.0%	10.7%
4. Cigar and cigarette use	11.6%	19.8%	14.7%
5. Alcohol use	29.7%	37.4%	21.5%
6. Physically forced to have sex	5.4%	21.9%	13.1%
7. Used electronic vape product	42.8%	50.5%	37.3%
8. Felt sad or hopeless	27.5%	63.0%	46.4%
9. Marijuana use	19.1%	30.6%	18.9%
10. Driving after drinking	5.2%	6.9%	9.5%
11. Experienced dating violence	6.4%	17.2%	14.1%
12. Threatened/ injured by weapon at school	5.4%	9.4%	11.1%

With such risk factors being associated with homosexual and bisexual behavior, parents have to stay connected with our children. That irreplaceable supportive relationship with us will help draw our children toward our Christian values rather than letting peers and the media influence them to accept values that are not biblical.

Evaluating Your Own Views of Homosexuality

To maintain a relationship with a teen who is struggling with any issue related to homosexuality, you may need to examine your own fears and feelings about the subject. If a teen tells us that he or she is exploring the subject—either because of "gay" friends or wondering if they themselves are homosexual—you may have a strong emotional reaction. Why? Let's examine the reasons you might feel this way. Does your immediate family's attitudes or even the media affect your view of the subject? Did you have previous negative experiences with homosexuality, perhaps even a homosexual encounter in your past or abuse by someone of your own gender? Have you been taunted or accused of being homosexual? Do you believe homosexuality is a more serious sin than other kinds of sin? If any of these statements are true for you, you need to address your own concerns about homosexuality before you will be effective in addressing the homosexual concerns of teens.

Isn't it a bit ironic that we fear broaching homosexuality with our teens? Yet if the teen brings up homosexuality, we are also immediately uptight and uncomfortable. If we are uncomfortable discussing the subject, teens will find other sources of information—often from individuals who will encourage them to pursue a homosexual lifestyle. We want to be the ones having conversations with our teens about this, as with the other topics in this book, because we bring a biblical perspective to the subject.

In teaching our teens to treat others with respect and dignity, we should set firm boundaries about how homosexuality is discussed in our homes and our churches. There should be no tolerance of gay jokes or insults or innuendoes. If we have teens who are struggling with homosexuality or are being labeled as homosexual in youth groups or their circles of acquaintance, we need to make every effort to ensure that they are being treated with compassion and respect. Similarly, we need to recognize that our teens may likely already have friends who are homosexual.

What Does the Bible Say?

Some prominent people claim that homosexual behavior is not sinful. Dr. Scott and I have a high view of the Bible as both authoritative and timeless in its messages. We offer these thoughts for parents to consider, and as appropriate, to share with their teens (but don't dump it all on them at once!).

The God of the Bible who walked around on this earth—Jesus—did not directly address the subject of homosexuality in any of His lessons, it's true. And Pharisees accurately said of Him that He associated with, and treated kindly, all types of sinful people. However, despite His silence on homosexuality (and a lot of other behavioral issues), Jesus insisted that He and His Father were in complete agreement on everything, and there are several strong and unmistakable warnings about homosexual behavior that Jesus' Father has made through the ages. They include, "You shall not lie with a male as with a woman; it is an abomination" (Leviticus 18:22 ESV), and, "If a man has sexual relations with a man as one does with a woman, both of them have done what is detestable" (Leviticus 20:13). These prohibitions were both civil laws and behavioral laws. The fact that condemnation of homosexual behavior is not just part of an old Jewish law code is seen in Romans 1:26–27, where homosexuality is described as a sign of corruption and rebellion against God:

> Because of this, God gave them over to shameful lusts. Even their women exchanged natural sexual relations for unnatural ones. In the same way the men also abandoned natural relations with women and were inflamed with lust for one another. Men committed shameful acts with other men, and received in themselves the due penalty for their error.

But there's also a visible demonstration of why homosexuality isn't part of God's approved plan for sexual relations. Males and females weren't created to have sex with their own genders. Even a teen can see this: A man's body and a woman's body quite literally fit together in ways that male-male and female-female sex could never do. When God created woman, He crafted her body to be "appropriate" for a man. Penises and vaginas are evidence: Male and female bodies fit together for three purposes—for simultaneous mutual pleasure, for bonding that validates long-term relationships, and for keeping the human race going.

God is a God of order. He made species, such as ducks and lizards, unable to procreate together. He made men+men and women+women unable to procreate as well. (No, adoption, in vitro fertilization, and surrogate mothering aren't outside of God's approved plan—they simply depend on third parties and/or technology to do what a male+female union naturally does.) But not only can homosexual unions not reproduce, they can inherently never be as satisfying in any way as is obedience to the God who created human bodies. Ongoing sin never fixes anything.

Homosexual behavior is a sin. But what about homosexual attraction? Unfortunately, your teen didn't get to "choose" his or her vulnerabilities, weaknesses, or inclinations to sin. Did you choose your overeating habits? Your daily struggles against porn, wasteful shopping trips, internet addiction, susceptibility to alcohol, pride, jealousy, or other things that you hate in your own character? Sexual sins are a special class, Paul says, because with them we sin against our own bodies (1 Corinthians 6:18), but many people didn't choose those other kinds of sins and must fight them every day of their lives.

If your teen is struggling with same-sex attraction, he or she may have the same type of lifelong struggles you do with your sins. This is hard for parents to accept, but in some cases that attraction may never change. Many people continue to feel these attractions and must exercise self-control. Some find that it was only a phase and go on to satisfying lifelong heterosexual relations. But some don't ever develop sexual feelings toward the opposite gender. For them, there's no "cure" or change.

Christian writer Christopher Yuan said of escaping his homosexual actions of the past, "I had always thought that the opposite of homosexuality was heterosexuality. But actually the opposite of homosexuality is holiness."[4]

You are called to help your teenager achieve holiness, that is, a relationship with the God who designed every human being's body by knitting it together in their mother's womb. He designed your daughter's body that way. He designed your son's body that way.

But the passage in Romans 1 that condemns homosexuality also warns us as parents against what could be called "the sin of applause" in verse 32: "Although they know God's righteous decree that those who do such things deserve death, they not only continue to do these very things but also approve of those who practice them." All sin separates us from God and leads to spiritual death. The key for you is to show love and acceptance of your child, no matter what his or her sin might be, while keeping the sacred trust of parenting that requires you to tell your child what God requires and why you will support what He says and not applaud sin.

Your Part

The single most important thing a parent needs to remember in discussing homosexuality is to do everything you can to foster communication and loving relationship while also making sure your child knows what God teaches about homosexuality and other sexual sins.

Let's return to the scenario from the beginning of this chapter, in which a mom is worried about her child's friendship with someone who believes herself to be homosexual. While parents might prefer to totally isolate teens from any sexual promiscuity outside of marriage, that's not realistic in our world. Here are some suggestions to help your children who have friends struggling with homosexuality.

Don't focus on sexuality. If teens are going to have relationships with friends struggling with homosexuality, they need to strategize to keep the focus of the relationship on shared interests and activities, rather than letting the entire relationship focus on the homosexuality of the friend. Help your teens realize that the other friendships they have do not focus on sexuality and neither should this one. While it is okay to discuss their friend's emotional reactions, it is not okay to be discussing their friend's sexual encounters or fantasies.

Set boundaries. Help teens think about the boundaries of the relationship, especially the clear bright lines about physical contact and spending time alone. The same rules would apply as in a heterosexual situation—stay away from touches and settings that make sinning easier. Our children and their friends need to stay in public areas in our household and in other households. We adults don't take our friends into our bedrooms, and our teens shouldn't take their friends into their bedrooms or other private spaces in homes.

Don't go there. While teens can continue to interact with friends struggling with homosexuality, they shouldn't enter into the activities of the gay community. Such activities—parades, awareness events, fundraisers, meetings—will pressure teens to change their views on homosexuality. Teens frequently do not have the decision-making and coping skills to handle this type of challenge to their faith. Similarly, teens don't have the skills to help friends who are struggling with homosexuality.

Know right from wrong. If teens begin to seriously question biblical teachings about homosexuality, they may not be able to maintain their friendship with someone struggling with homosexuality. You be the model in this: Like you, teens need to clearly articulate their beliefs and recognize that they can show love and kindness and respect while still honoring God's teachings.

Ask for help. Teens need to have adults they can talk to about their friendship and how it is affecting them—adults who will listen, be supportive, and hold them to biblical standards of conduct. The most important way to ask for help is to turn to God. Teens may have to stop talking with their friends about the subject or even end the friendship. However, teens need to know that if they let it go, God will handle it. Encourage teens to pray for their friends struggling with sin. Help them see that God loves their friends more than they do and that He will hear their prayers.

Your Teen Asks, "Am I Gay?"

When a teen tells you that he or she is struggling with homosexuality, you need more information before you respond. You can assess the situation and provide teens with accurate information without operating on stereotypes. People—adults and teens alike—often think they can "spot" a homosexual, but they're often wrong! For instance:

- "You can tell someone is homosexual by how they dress." How someone dresses does not indicate their sexual orientation; it indicates their taste in clothing and style.

- "You can tell someone is homosexual by how they act." If a female is interested in "tomboy" activities or a male is interested in typically feminine activities, it does not mean they are homosexual, but rather shows a lack of conformity to cultural gender roles.
- "If teens are confused about their sexual feelings, they are homosexual." Confusion about sexual issues is a typical developmental stage for adolescents.
- "You are homosexual if members of the opposite sex don't show a sexual interest in you." Sometimes teens have other interpersonal problems or the teen just hasn't met the right person yet.
- "If you look at the bodies of people of the same sex, you must be homosexual." Looking at the bodies of members of the same sex may be about trying to establish identity or trying to establish a standard for physical appearance. It isn't necessarily about homosexual attraction.

In addition, teens may inaccurately believe they are homosexual for several reasons:

- *Sexual abuse.* Teens who have been sexually abused by an adult of the same sex may believe that they are homosexual. They inaccurately believe that perpetrators were attracted to their homosexual tendencies or that an abuse experience will define their sexual orientation for the rest of their lives.
- *Gender-role issues.* Males who enjoy typically female activities or females who enjoy typically male activities may believe that these interests define them as homosexual. Engaging in activities that are typical of the

opposite sex is not related to whether a person is homosexual or heterosexual.

- *Name-calling.* Teens who have been harassed by peers and called derogatory names suggesting they are homosexual may believe that they are homosexual. These teens may believe that other people recognize they are homosexual, even if they don't believe they are. Other people don't define sexual orientation for teens.

- *Sexual experimentation.* Teens may have had some sexual contact with a peer of the same sex. While this is certainly wrong, incidents of sexual experimentation do not define someone's sexual orientation.

- *Homosexual friends.* Teens with friends who identify themselves as homosexual may believe they are homosexual, especially if they did not recognize that their friends were homosexual.

- *Homosexual advances.* Teens who have had someone who is homosexual try to come on to them may believe that they are homosexual, but a homosexual person who reveals their physical and/or sexual interest in you does not define your sexuality.

- *Emotional vulnerability.* Teens who are experiencing a life crisis (death in the family, chronic illness in the family, parental divorce) may be emotionally vulnerable. At such times, they will seek emotional support wherever they find it. If that emotional support comes from someone who is the same sex or someone who is homosexual, they may identify themselves as homosexual.

- *Exposure to pornography.* Teens who have been exposed to pornographic materials may have seen or heard things that have changed their perceptions about sexuality and members of the same sex or the opposite sex, leading them to conclude they are homosexual.

- *Poor sense of identity.* Teens may not have a clear understanding of their personal identity and may be influenced by media, peers, or adults to believe that they will find more gratification in a homosexual relationship than in a heterosexual relationship.

What Can a Parent Do?

If you are the parent of a teen struggling with homosexuality or bisexuality, you need to aggressively seek out people who will support you as you walk through this difficult journey with your teen. You will need friends who will fall to their knees and pray with you, and friends who will wrap their arms around you and anchor you when you feel lost. You will also need friends who will hold you accountable for how you navigate a difficult situation. Remember, your primary job is to prepare your children for heaven. You have to keep God close and help your children understand how much you and God love them.

Help your teens stay connected with godly people who will encourage them to make good choices. If teens disconnect from their church family, they will certainly develop connections in the homosexual community. When teens find primary support in a group that encourages and affirms choices that are not biblical, they will make many more decisions based on inaccurate information and peer pressure than they will make based on what God wants them to do. Similarly, help teens study the Bible and seek out reliable videos and other resources so they can clearly understand their relationship with God and His plan for sexuality.

Teens may feel ashamed and embarrassed about their sexual struggles. Your teen has taken a big risk in telling you about struggling with homosexuality. Telling you about these struggles is an expression of deep trust. Honor the trust your teen has placed in you by keeping his or her confidences and not identifying these struggles publicly. Over and over, remind him or her that everyone struggles with sin (including you!) and that you don't get to pick your own temptations. Just because our society places a stigma on homosexuality doesn't mean God considers it an unforgivable sin. We are not defined by our sins!

Whatever you do, don't let all the interactions you have with teens focus on their struggles with homosexuality. Try to have fun with your teens. Recognize that they need to feel connection with you and enjoy being around you. Strategize and brainstorm activities you can enjoy together and spend time with your teens. Your time and attention are the most important gifts you can give your teens. Validate their sense of worth by investing time with them.

As you consider what to do to help your teen deal with homosexuality, recognize that there will be situations in which you need the help of a professional counselor to help you and your child deal with the struggle. If the answer to any of the following questions is yes, then you may need to refer the teen to a professional counselor.

- Has the teen tried to stop the homosexual activity but has failed to quit?
- Is the teen getting more involved in the homosexual community?
- Is the teen in a committed homosexual relationship?
- Is the teen receiving significant support from adults for homosexual choices?
- Is the teen significantly depressed or suicidal?
- Is the teen engaging in self-mutilation?
- Is the teen withdrawing from the youth group and other peers?
- Is the teen engaging in delinquent behaviors?

Final Words

Your teens may not always make the choices you want them to make, but no matter what choice they make, your role is to point them back to God. Lecturing them or condemning them is not going to accomplish that. At the end of time, when we meet God shoulder to shoulder with our matured children, we will answer for what we did to bring them closer to Him or drive them away from Him. When our teens are vulnerable and struggling, when we don't know what else to do, we can love fiercely and make sure our kids know we love them. Our model in this is Jesus' interactions with sinners on earth. He showed great compassion for people who were honestly struggling with sin.

We can remind our teens that the Creator of all human bodies lived in one himself on earth. This is not theoretical for Him, it's practical. He knew the realities of the sins of others and yet didn't join in those sins. He could love fiercely and yet hold the line on things He knew were harmful for all of us. He knows your son or daughter inside and out and loves them enough to sacrifice His own body for them. That's genuine love.

EXPLORATION
WITH YOUR TEEN

Question from teen: "What do I do if someone asks me what I think of homosexuality?"

Parent response:

- What do you think the word *homosexual* means? (Be prepared to talk openly about homosexual behavior.)

- Let's look at Genesis 2:18, where God said He created the first woman, Eve, for the first man, Adam: "The LORD God said, 'It is not good for the man to be alone. I will make a helper suitable for him.'" God also told the couple to "be fruitful and increase in number" (Genesis 1:28)—which implies they would have sex. How was the woman "suitable" for the man in the sense of being sexually appropriate? How does this couple show God's ideal for sexual relations?

- Look at this verse from Leviticus 18:22: "Do not have sexual relations with a man as one does with a woman; that is detestable." What does the word *detestable* mean? What do you think it means to "have sexual relations with a man as one does a woman"?

- Read Romans 1:26–27, where God's anger about homosexuality is described: "Women exchanged natural sexual relations for unnatural ones. In the same way the men also abandoned natural relations with women and were inflamed with lust for one another. Men committed shameful acts with other men, and received in themselves the due penalty for their error." (Ask, "What do you think God thinks about homosexuality?" Be prepared to explain any terms in this passage such as "natural sexual relations" and "due penalty," for example.)

Question from teen: "The Bible says not to judge. So why should I think homosexuality is bad?"

Parent response:

- Let's read Matthew 7:1 together: "Do not judge, or you too will be judged." Is this verse saying not to judge at all? (Remind your teen that everyone wants to be treated fairly. But it's not saying not to judge; the next verse goes on to say, "For in the same way you judge others, you will be judged, and with the measure you use, it will be measured to you.")

- What would happen in your life if you weren't allowed to make any choices about what you see as good or bad? What do you know about God that might make you think He knows what's good and what's bad? "God is a fair judge, a God who is angered by injustice every day. If a person does not change, God sharpens his sword" (Psalm 7:11–12 GW).

- What does this verse mean: "Stop judging by mere appearances, but instead judge correctly" (John 7:24). Does this verse say not to judge at all? What should be the basis for a Christian to judge if something is good or bad? (Point out that the individual heart can't be the basis for judgment because millions of people may have another opinion. But we have information from the One who designed the human body.)

Question from your son: "My friend just told me he's gay. What should I do?"

Parent response:

- What do you think your friend wants you to do? Is it possible he is interested in you? Or could he be wondering if he's doing something wrong and might need support in walking through this? Can you stand up for truth? Read James 5:19–20: "My brothers and sisters, if one of you should wander from the truth and someone should bring that person back, remember this: Whoever turns a sinner from the error of their way will save them from death and cover over a multitude of sins."

- What might be the good results of staying friends with someone who is genuinely struggling with homosexuality? (Loyalty, support—"A friend loves at all times, and a brother is born for a time of adversity" (Proverbs 17:17).

- What might be bad results? (Your child might be labeled homosexual as well; might be taunted or bullied, or could be drawn into homosexual attitudes or practices. First Corinthians 15:33 says, "Do not be misled: 'Bad company corrupts good character.'" Ask: Will being close to this friend be worth those risks? Will it help you do what Philippians 4:8 says: "Whatever is true, whatever is noble, whatever is right, whatever is pure, whatever is lovely, whatever is admirable—if anything is excellent or praiseworthy—think about such things"?

TWELVE

Understanding Gender Issues

Mackenna was an articulate and bright homeschooled teen who dressed in typically feminine styles and had long blond hair. So it startled her parents when, a couple of months ago, she cut her hair short and colored it a darker shade and began wearing men's jeans and T-shirts she bought at thrift stores.

She moved from the center of youth group activities to the fringes, and she and two other girls began discussing sexual orientation and gender issues. Soon they started their own Bible study group. Her concerned parents asked me to see Mackenna in counseling. The first time I meet with her, she is quick to tell me that she's not the one who needs counseling.

"It's my parents who need it. They don't like my friends and how I am changing, but this is what I want to do."

"I'm a little confused—what do you want to do?"

"I have this friend, Ardyn, at church, who feels like she is a boy who has always been trapped in a girl's body, even from when she was little. Now she wears guy clothes and has a guy's haircut." Mackenna unconsciously smooths her own short hair, and I see passion rising in her face. "But the other kids in the youth group are making fun of her. She is scared and lonely. I don't want her to feel so left out."

"So you changed how you look because you don't want your friend to feel left out?"

"A couple of my friends and I noticed how alone Ardyn seemed at youth group, and we heard the mean things other kids were saying, so we decided that we would become her friends and dress like her so that she didn't feel so alone."

"Wow! I appreciate your compassion for her, but why haven't you explained this to your parents?"

"I don't really know." She juts her chin. "I didn't think about talking to them at first, then they got so weird about it and I didn't want them to keep me from hanging out with Ardyn. The last thing she needs right now is to lose friends in the youth group. Her parents make her come to the youth group because they think it will convince her she's not a guy."

"So . . . you didn't tell your parents because you thought they would make you quit your friendship with Ardyn?"

"They got so weird on me! They made some remarks about my guy clothes at first, but they never asked me what was going on. They just made up their minds about what I was doing. They whispered to each other and talked a lot in their bedroom. I know they were talking about me, so I just decided that I would stay quiet and let them think what they were going to think."

How Prevalent Is Transgender?

While gender issues are drawing a lot of attention in the media and on social media, the reality is that only about 2 percent of high school students identify as transgender.[1] Ardyn's experience with her peers' reaction is common: The small number of high school students who identify as transgender are bullied and harassed more than other teens.[2] There's a trickle-down effect: As a result of bullying and harassment, transgender students are at greater risk of using alcohol, marijuana, and other drugs,[3] and 35 percent of students who identify as transgender have attempted suicide in the last year.[4]

So while very few teens actually identify as having gender issues, teens are much more aware of transgender issues. According to a recent Barna report, more teens today (37 percent) say their gender and sexuality is an important part of their sense of self, compared with their parents (28 percent).[5] "About a third of teens know someone who is transgender, and the majority (69 percent) say it's acceptable to be born one gender and to feel like another."[6]

Gender fluidity (the idea that the authentic self is not connected to biology, and that body and behavior can thus be altered as desired) is a subject not directly addressed in Scripture. Like nuclear warfare, carbon footprints, stem cell research, and genetic engineering, we have to infer what's right from what the Bible says in general principles that are true across all millennia. But unlike those just-mentioned new social issues, the Bible is explicit about enough of the do's and don'ts of sexuality for you to know right from wrong. You'll need stories and concepts to catch your teen's attention, and bedrock realities to anchor them.

They see cultural icons like young Jazz, marked a boy from birth, who has an enormous social media presence as a girl. And one of the largest cosmetic firms in the world uses makeup models born as boys. Your teen may read with you Deuteronomy 22:5 ("A woman must not wear men's clothing, nor a man wear women's clothing, for the LORD your God detests anyone who does this"), and be assured the "trans" culture will help them ask you questions.

Gender Terms

If you're going to talk to anyone about gender, you need to be on the same page with terms about gender and understand how non-Christians and others would define them. You and I might disagree with how someone might define a term, but you need to know what others are talking about. The list provided can be a starting point for a conversation with your teen. You could ask how your teen uses a term, for instance.

As we've already seen in the chapter about sexual orientation, you can't assess someone just by observation. Remember, gender is not the same as orientation. Gender is a person's assessment of their identity. Orientation is the way they relate to other genders and types.

- Androgynous: Identifying and/or presenting with masculine and feminine characteristics; may not be able to distinguish masculine or feminine characteristics.

- Bisexual: A person emotionally and/or sexually attracted in a romantic way to more than one sex, gender, or gender identity. The attractions may not be simultaneous or to the same degree.

- Cisgender: A person's gender identity is consistent with birth sex.

- Gender dysphoria: Distress caused when a person's gender identity is not the same as birth sex.

- Gender expression: Methods of expressing masculinity or femininity through behavior, clothing, haircut, or voice. These expressions of femininity and masculinity might not align with defined social expressions of gender.

- Gender-fluid: A person who does not identify with being either male or female, but has or expresses a fluid gender identity.

- Gender identity: A person's internal concept of self as being male, female, or a blend of both or neither. Gender identity can be the same or different from the sex assigned at birth.

- Gender transition: The process by which some people socially transition to another gender. They might begin dressing and using names and pronouns of another gender. Some individuals may go through a physical transition to medically transform their bodies to another gender.

- Non-binary: A person who does not identify as a man or a woman. Non-binary people may identify as being both a man and a woman, as somewhere in between, or as neither.

- Queer: Individuals who generally reject notions of static categories of gender and sexual orientation. They may see themselves as neither male nor female, or as both male and female. These individuals embrace a fluidity of gender identity and sometimes sexual orientation.

- Transgender: Individuals whose gender identity and/ or expression is different from cultural expectations for their birth sex. Being transgender does not imply any specific sexual orientation.

Making Sense of Gender Confusion

When Dr. Scott was researching a book about archaeology, her coauthor handed her the rim of an ancient pot from the excavations of biblical Sodom.[7] The outside of the shard had endured a near hit from an airburst meteor nearly four thousand years ago. There, on the inside surface of the pot, was the distinct fingerprint of the potter who made it. That pot was made by that person, and the fingerprint proved it.

The same is true for each human body, a wondrous work of art that is on a becoming-eternal journey. Each body bears fingerprints of its Creator (such as intelligence, communication, and the housing of a soul). One of those indelible fingerprints is gender. This started with the first division of cells after the joyful meeting up of a sperm and an egg. Every cell in that body from that point on had the identification of one sex or another. That can't be changed. You can lie to your body and tell it that it doesn't know what it is, but it will always hold up a banner: *DNA doesn't lie.* You can mutilate it and add to it and pump it full of drugs and dress it up, but it won't change the cell-deep reality.

Personhood isn't the outward appearance. It's a package deal: body plus soul. This package yearns for unity. The soul's most basic need is for unity with God.[8] There is eternity in our hearts,[9] and to paraphrase a statement by Pascal, there is a God-shaped vacuum in the heart of each person. And the body yearns for redemption, for a joyful meeting up with its Creator in heaven in a resurrected form.

With those bedrock understandings under your belt, you also should keep reminding yourself of the difference between gender identity and sexual orientation. Remember from the last chapter, while sexual orientation describes sexual attraction, gender identity describes a person's internal sense of being male or female. Although the overwhelming majority of people have a gender identity that matches their anatomy, there are people who believe that their gender identity does not match their anatomy.

Your Skill Set for Talking to Your Teen

- One of your preparations in talking to your child about gender fluidity is that you should be unabashed in describing sex-change surgery and hormone treatments and how these sexual crutches can be irreversible.
- You have to be aware that subtle linguistic changes are happening to persuade your child that it's right to seek identity with a different behavior or anatomy. For instance, the mutilation of the body is now called "gender *confirmation* surgery"—to carry the idea that the body didn't know what it was and must be altered to match or confirm what the mind thinks it is.
- Those who don't respect the Bible can be very persuasive in using specific Scriptures to sow doubt in the receptive mind of your teen. They may say that since Jesus didn't address homosexuality or gender fluidity, that means it couldn't be a sin. They may use Galatians 3:28 ("There is neither Jew nor Gentile, neither slave nor free, nor is there male and female, for you are all one in Christ Jesus") to advance the idea that one's sexual identity isn't important. However, your teen should be able to clearly see that only a woman's ovaries produce eggs and only testicles can produce sperm. Bodies and their functions are not interchangeable.

God and Identity

God is very adamant about identity. He told the Israelites over and over that it wasn't just any power, not a golden calf or weather event or anything, that brought them out of slavery. Exodus 20:2, the first of the Ten Commandments—"I am the Lord your God"—warns about errors or misrepresentations about who He is.

He is equally careful about people's identities. Since He creates each individual, crafting with personality and uniqueness, He protects His intentions against identity theft and marks people as male or female.

"Wait a minute," a transgender advocate might say. "What about people who are born with indistinct genitalia?" Often this question can be resolved with genetic testing. There are some cases of true physical androgeny or indistinct genitalia, but they are a very tiny percentage of people.

Furthermore, there's nothing new in this world about sexual mutilation. People have been lopping off women's breasts and labia for thousands of years. And the practice of castrating males is not only ancient, it's directly addressed in the Bible. Such men are called eunuchs, and Jesus *does* talk about them in Matthew 19:12: "For there are eunuchs who were born that way, and there are eunuchs who have been made eunuchs by others—and there are those who choose to live like eunuchs for the sake of the kingdom of heaven. The one who can accept this should accept it." So here Jesus addresses three conditions: androgeny from birth, victims of sexual mutilation, and the voluntarily celibate. All were not just tolerated but welcome in God's kingdom. All should live under the same rule of holy sexual behavior. These words of Jesus were the stabbing of light into ancient darkness on this subject.

That is not to say that Christians themselves have not muddied the waters about sexual identity and using culture to define what is "manly" and what is "womanly" in the past. Christianity is timeless and not culture-bound, even though it originated in a particular culture at a particular time. In most cultures, women are child-bearers and nurturers and men do other work. However, insisting that anyone who is male must swagger and male children must play sports or have more active toys, and that anyone who is female must be demure and female children must play house isn't fair.

We have to leave room for godly personalities that don't fit all gender rules. Men who are kind and tender and nurturing are no less men, and women who are strong and protective are no less women, and teens need to hear that truth from their parents.[10] They also need to see it in the attitudes of those parents toward anyone struggling with gender identity.

There can be no doubt that organized, purposeful, and well-funded organizations exist to get you and your child to accept gender fluidity. You may think that this is a battle so overwhelming and so multifaceted in this community (LGBTQ+ in which the plus can mean an alphabet soup of anything from omnisexual to asexual) that you can't fight it. But its chaos is beginning to show cracks. Mental health professionals,[11] homosexuals,[12] and feminists[13]—all of whom had at one point seemed to embrace transsexuals—now do not. And young people are showing their reluctance too.

For a young person, announcing that you're *becoming* transsexual can be a path to popularity with enormous support, especially on social media. But actually *being* a transsexual is often a path to loneliness. A recent study found that the overwhelming majority of people (90 percent, including members of the LGBTQ+ community) don't want to date a transsexual.[14] There are numerous studies online that show that attempts to change one's sex leads to increased stress.

Your teen won't know these things from the media. Nor do you have to confront your teen with this. It may be enough for you to know that sexual sin and its supporters are not a giant, monolithic structure.

You are undoubtedly aware that opposition to "trans"—choosing one's sexual identity—is seen as prejudice, the same as opposition to someone of another race. But if one's maleness or femaleness is assigned unmistakably by God before birth, isn't it as logical to call opposition to that reality a kind of prejudice? For a culture that puts a high premium on scientific findings, it's pretty hard to get around the fact that inherent maleness and inherent femaleness at a cellular level are documented and unchangeable. That's a deal breaker for people other than Christians too.

Final Words

Gender issues have emerged in teen culture so rapidly that there has been little time for research to develop studies on long-term outcomes of gender confusion and other issues related to gender. With limited duration and research on the impact of a culture that encouraged children and teens to explore and experiment with their gender identification, there is just no way to predict how individuals will identify their gender as they age. But we can take insight from how some former homosexuals look at their pasts. One former lesbian, Rosaria Butterfield, who is now a Christian, echoes the words of a seventy-five-year-old woman who, like her, had lived much of her life as gay and then heard the Gospel. "I understand that I may lose everything. Why didn't anyone tell me this before? Why did people I love not tell me that I would someday have to choose like this?"[15]

Somebody has to say the truth. Teens need real heroes who have made courageous, defendable decisions, like Rosaria Butterfield, who left her gay lifestyle for Christianity. But do you know what the "spark" was that got her to leave behind her partner, her academic career, and other things valuable to her? It wasn't arguments. It was the kindness and hospitality of a Christian couple who showed her love and respectfully presented the truth of the Bible.

Once you understand that gender exploration is a normal part of overall identity development—and you make sure you say so clearly to your teen—you can become a trusted guide for your teens and their friends as they navigate gender issues. Remember, their brains are still developing, and though they may not process information as you'd like, they will certainly understand kindness. They will accurately process a smile and a snack. A "safe place" for them is somewhere they get affirmation of their worth before God and the support they need as they support friends. You don't have to approve of every decision their friends make. If you communicate in a nonjudgmental way what the Bible teaches ("Have you considered this viewpoint about how God knits a soul and body together?" for example), combined with your demonstrable love and concern for your teens and their friends, you will open up opportunities to influence them all.

I've heard it said by parents of teens who are struggling, "I don't want to lose them." You don't have to. Kids who are battling with ideas about their bodies need places where they know they are safe and know that they will be loved, not judged. If we don't open our hearts and homes to struggling teens, in that emotional vacuum they will seek out places to belong, places that will endorse and encourage their confusion, places where people won't tell them about God's plan for their lives.

So that means your safe place *has* to include God's truth.

While you may not understand the gender confusion teens are experiencing, don't let your lack of knowledge turn into fear. Be the hands and feet of Jesus as we minister to our teens and their friends. While there is not a specific handbook for struggling with gender issues, there is a handbook for how to interact with other people—the Bible.

While I have tried to provide you with information in this chapter, I have only provided the basics you need to begin a conversation with your teen. As parents, we feel like we should know more than our kids, but this may be one situation where our teens know more than we do about what popular media is saying about gender identity. Let your teen see your curiosity and willingness to learn about their world. Ask questions and really listen to what your teen tells you.

God has called us to be the light in the midst of the world's darkness. There is no better place to begin than with our own children.

EXPLORATION
WITH YOUR TEEN

1. Memorizing Scriptures is a powerful way to help protect your child's sexual identity. Here are some good ones you should memorize along with them:

   - "Do you not know that your bodies are temples of the Holy Spirit, who is in you, whom you have received from God? You are not your own; you were bought at a price. Therefore honor God with your bodies" (1 Corinthians 6:19–20).
   - "For you created my inmost being; you knit me together in my mother's womb. I praise you because I am fearfully and wonderfully made; your works are wonderful, I know that full well" (Psalm 139:13–14).
   - And finally, to demonstrate that even "pre-Christians" (your teen if he or she hasn't made a commitment to Jesus Christ) are known and loved sacrificially by God:
   - "You see, at just the right time, when we were still powerless, Christ died for the ungodly. Very rarely

will anyone die for a righteous person, though for a good person someone might possibly dare to die. But God demonstrates his own love for us in this: While we were still sinners, Christ died for us" (Romans 5:6–8).

2. Ask your teen: From what you learn and observe in your science classes and in nature around you, is our Creator God random or purposeful?

3. Dialogue with your teen: If you were going to brainstorm some ways God could tell people that He lovingly and purposefully created them with a sexual identity and blessed it, what do you think He might say? Can you think of any Scriptures that show that?

4. Dialogue with your teen: If a person with anorexia looks in a mirror and sees someone who is disgustingly fat, how is that different from a male who looks in the mirror and says what he sees is not "the real him"?

5. One prominent atheist homosexual, Douglas Murray, says flatly that transsexuality is a lie. He speaks of the impossibility of "migrating between the sexes and that our bodies are like pieces of Lego—you can just stick bits onto it and if you don't like it you can take it off again."[16] Murray identifies this as a great moral issue because the trans community forces people who don't believe that someone born male can ever become a woman to say that such a person is no longer a man. Ask your teen: Have you felt pressure to lie about something you know as a fact, like the reality of your bodily, biological sex? How should a Christian handle this situation?

6. Ask your teen: How would knowing that God chose your gender bring you peace?

THIRTEEN

Unplanned and Unexpected

Julia, a sixteen-year-old girl with short, dark hair and intense eyes, sits in my office wringing her hands. She blurts out, "I think I might be pregnant, but I'm not sure."

"I know you are overwhelmed right now, but I need to know why you think you are pregnant."

"I'm nearly a month late," she manages to say. "I haven't started my period."

"Sometimes your period can be late without your being pregnant. Have you been having sex with someone?"

Julia's face flushes red with embarrassment as she stammers, "Well . . . um . . . not exactly."

"What do you mean not exactly?"

"Well, we haven't been actually doing it, but we've gotten pretty close to having sex." She goes on to describe mutual masturbation.

"Has your sexual partner—the guy—been ejaculating?"

Julia drops her eyes. "Yeah."

"Well, getting pregnant from that is possible but not probable. Have you taken a pregnancy test?"

"No."

We talk a bit more. I tell her that home pregnancy tests aren't always reliable, and that I will help her find a clinic that can do a free or low-cost test. She tells me that neither her parents nor her sixteen-year-old boyfriend know, and we discuss when or if to tell them.

A week later she calls to tell me the test was negative, and that she'd started her period the same day. I assure her that even though she's not pregnant now, any sexual contact where a male has ejaculated—whether with or without a condom or other forms of birth control—can result in pregnancy.

The Teen Pregnancy Landscape

You may be surprised to learn that teen pregnancies in the U.S. are at a record low. Although reasons for the declines are not totally clear, evidence suggests it's because more teens are abstaining from sexual activity, and the teens who are sexually active are using birth control more than in previous years. Still, the U.S. teen pregnancy rate is substantially higher than in other Western industrialized nations, and racial/ethnic and geographic disparities in teen birth rates persist.[1]

Most teen pregnancies are unintentional and unplanned. Generally, teens get pregnant either because they literally don't understand biologically how it is possible to get pregnant, or because they choose to engage in unprotected sex. Although teens are saturated with sexual messages in the media and the culture, very few of these messages give reliable information about how pregnancy occurs. For instance, characters in movies and television have sex with multiple partners often without any consequences of pregnancy.

It is hard to imagine that in our sex-saturated culture, some teens get pregnant because they don't understand how someone gets pregnant. Believe it or not, a common misperception among sexually active teens is that the only way you can get pregnant is to have oral sex. These teens believe that pregnancy occurs when a sperm is swallowed.

Teens sit in health classes and biology classes, but they have not connected the information they learned in health class with their behavior on dates. Perhaps one reason is the personal fable that makes them believe it won't happen to them. Perhaps they identify with celebrities they follow on social media who are sexually active but not getting pregnant. Whatever their thinking, they nonetheless sit in lectures about reproduction without connecting the "theoretical" discussions about sperm and eggs with their own vaginas and penises.

A second misperception related to pregnancy is that the only way you can get pregnant is by a penis penetrating a vagina. Teens are unaware that intimate sexual contact leading to ejaculation without penetration may result in pregnancy. A "splash pregnancy" occurs when seminal fluid penetrates the vaginal opening without vaginal intercourse. Once the seminal fluid enters the vagina, sperm can swim up through the female reproductive system and fertilize an egg, causing pregnancy. This can happen whether or not the male is wearing a condom, because condoms sometimes tear. Teens need to be aware that any time males ejaculate during sexual contact, there is a possibility for pregnancy to occur.

Planned Pregnancies

While most teen pregnancies are unplanned, it would be naïve to believe that all teen pregnancies are unplanned. Some teens strategize to get pregnant for any of the following reasons:

- *Escape.* Teens may want to leave their parents' homes, and pregnancy is viewed as a way to establish independence from their parents.

- *Abuse*. Teens may get pregnant to stop a perpetrator from sexually abusing them. One in ten teen pregnancies is the result of a sexual assault, usually incest.[2]
- *Affection*. Teens may want unconditional love, and they believe that a baby will love them that way.
- *Entrapment*. Teens may get pregnant because they want to marry their sexual partner and believe that if they get pregnant, their sexual partner will marry them.
- *Status*. In certain groups of teens, having children is a way to establish status. Teen parents are respected for their virility within some groups.

Knowing What to Do

Take responsibility. Teens who are pregnant will have to make significant decisions about the life of a child. Whether teens choose abortion, adoption, or raising the child, there are significant, enduring consequences to their decisions.

Real parenting. If teens believe that they want to raise the child themselves, they need to have a realistic idea of the demands of parenting. Parenting classes and counsel from adult parents can provide a realistic picture of taking care of a child twenty-four hours a day.

Selective inclusion. While a teen may think she can continue her schooling and social life relatively unchanged until a baby's birth, sometimes physical limitations (morning sickness, changes in size and flexibility) and safety concerns from a school will limit activities. Girls often romanticize parenting as glorified babysitting and are shocked to learn that they either can't participate or aren't invited as they previously were to many activities.

Connection with other parents. Perhaps more than ever in her life, a pregnant teen needs guidance in making connections with other Christian parents who can mentor her and include her in new social situations. Since our culture does not place any stigma on premarital sex and having children outside a marriage relationship, it is usually a shock for a teen mother to discover that her old friends and social activities can almost disappear.

All or nothing. If a young woman wants to raise a child herself, she may not recognize the enormity of such a responsibility. A part of my counseling practice is working with custody conflicts. This is an unpleasant but true statement: *Almost always when grandparents or other family members assume a great deal of the responsibility for raising the child, it eventually creates significant conflicts between the teen and the grandparents.* Families split apart in custody battles over children or over disagreements in parenting. For that reason, if a teen cannot parent the child herself, I urge grandparents or other family members to either take legal custody of the child or encourage the teen to find a family to adopt the child.

Acceptance, not endorsement. Teens who are pregnant certainly need support from their physical and church families, but we need to balance the need for support for their material and spiritual needs against the unrealistic glamorizing of pregnancy that gives other young women the impression that starting a new family without marriage is anything but a great misfortune that must be avoided at all costs.

Acknowledgment of wrongdoing. A pregnant teen must come to the conclusion and acknowledge that engaging in premarital sex is wrong. Without such an acknowledgement of wrongdoing, teens may see nothing wrong with their actions and feel permitted to repeat them. (The exception to this would be if the teen was forced to engage in nonconsensual sex.)

Abortion

While abortion receives a lot of attention, especially as a political issue, you may be surprised to learn some downward trends.[3]

The decrease in abortion rates is approximately a 70 percent reduction. The reasons for this decline are not clear, but the following are some possible reasons:

Contraception has become more accessible and as a result, teens are not having as many unplanned pregnancies.[4]

Declining teen sexual activity could also be contributing to lower rates of abortion. Research shows a long-term increase in the number of people in the United States—mostly younger men—reporting not having sex in the past year. Other data show that the proportion of high school students who have ever had sexual intercourse declined between 2011 and 2017, with most of the decline happening in the 2013–2015 period.[5]

When It Gets Personal

I know a woman who grew up in a Christian home, but she was quite rebellious. She began dating a young man her parents disapproved of, and despite their protests, she continued her relationship with him. After a few months, they eloped so they could be married immediately. She was seventeen and he was nineteen.

From their wedding night it was obvious she had made a terrible mistake, for it was then that the physical violence began. As she sat, bruised and shaking, she knew that her parents' worst predictions had come true. But in a matter of days she was a thousand miles away, living in a small town in New Mexico.

The words of her parents rang in her ears daily: "There has never been a divorce in our family." When she telephoned to tell her parents where she was, they responded, "You made your bed. Now lie in it."

And she tried to, as best she could.

There were few happy times. Her husband's fits of rage soon led her to a conclusion that would eventually be vindicated, though years later: He was mentally ill.

And then the worst thing of all happened. She found herself pregnant.

She was desperate. She knew even then that children in such a marriage would be abused too. Had abortions been available in that time, years ago, she says she would have unhesitatingly sought one.

The child was born, and another. Her fears were realized. His rages began to focus at times on the children. His presence in the home was one of unpredictable moods, violent outbursts, betrayals, and recriminations.

It was seventeen long years before she saved up enough money to file for divorce. And even then, she was alone: Because of her husband's illness, she never received a penny of alimony or child support to raise the two teenagers and the toddler they had.

When that woman tells of her hurt, her desperation each time she found out she was pregnant, she is not exaggerating. I know that all her fears came true.

The first child born into that situation was my coauthor, Dr. Scott. She has quite a personal take on abortion.

"You see, the questions about issues of such things as when life begins are to me somewhat relative to a greater personal reality," Dr. Scott says. "I am puzzled by the thinking that any of us knows enough about the long-term future to be willing to kill to avert it.

"And the matter of when life begins is much less important to me than this truth: *We each only have one life.* The Bible puts it this way: 'It is appointed for a man once to die, and then the judgment.' If the Bible is true, then there is no reincarnation, no 'do-overs' on living.

"My childhood wasn't a great childhood, but it was my only childhood. It stands in my life as the great witness to the truth of Romans 8:28, that God will work all things for good.

"Simply put," Dr. Scott says, "I'd rather have lived than not have lived."

The Pros and Cons of Abortion

I know parents who were staunchly anti-abortion who changed their mind about abortion when their own daughters became pregnant. But abortion is a short-term solution to a difficult problem. Pregnancy causes parents to foresee, usually accurately, a future for their daughter that can realistically preclude high school graduation, college, or career aspirations. With an abortion, teens don't have to deal with the emotional and physical consequences of pregnancy. They don't have to choose between adoptive parents or raising a child as a single parent. With an abortion, the pregnant teen doesn't have to maintain a relationship with the father of the child or include the father of the child in decisions being made about the child. Parents know well how expensive the birth process is, and that's just the start of enormous financial responsibility for at least two decades. And such parents often assure the pregnant teen that their own busy lives wouldn't allow them to raise another child. Then there's the shame and the emotional implications of having an unplanned child and the necessary 24/7 care. An unplanned pregnancy hijacks your life. These are all serious, compelling reasons parents and a daughter would consider an abortion.

Notice that the previous justifications given for abortion certainly are taking into consideration the enormous costs of a pregnancy—financial, social, physical, and emotional—to a teenage girl and her family. However, although these reasons express great compassion and protectiveness for the young woman, they are not biblically based reasons.[6]

I do not believe that God accepts abortion as a solution to an unwanted pregnancy.[7] There are several reasons why. Look at all the Scriptures throughout this book showing that God carefully and individually created each of us. The God of the Bible is concerned for every person He crafted, but is especially protective of the weak, the defenseless, and the innocent. Surely that describes babies.[8] And the Bible portrays life as a gift to humans, not something they can take from another human for their own convenience.

One of the most convicting proofs of the awareness and personhood of children in the womb is in Luke 1:41–44. Mary, newly pregnant, went to visit her cousin Elizabeth, who was also pregnant. As soon as Mary's voice called out in greeting, the pre-born John the Baptist literally jumped for joy in Elizabeth's uterus. If a regular human baby does that in the womb, how can you say he is not human? That you can take his life without spiritual consequences? Surely your teen needs to know this, soul-deep, before she would consider trading away the life of her unborn child.[9]

Sexually Transmitted Diseases

Another unpleasant side effect of teenage sexual behavior (both heterosexual and other varieties) is a totally preventable and sometimes lifelong and/or life-threatening disease. While teen pregnancy seems to be declining, that's certainly not the case with sexually transmitted diseases.[10] Though STDs affect individuals of all ages, they take a particularly heavy toll on young people. The CDC estimates that youth ages fifteen to twenty-four "make up just over one quarter of the sexually active population, but account for half of the 20 million new sexually transmitted infections that occur in the United States each year."[11]

These statistics show that your teen is much more likely to get an STD—which may affect his or her entire physical health and social relations for a lifetime—than they are to get pregnant or seek an abortion. Schools recognize this, so a great deal of attention in sex education of teens has been focused on sexually transmitted diseases (to the neglect, I think, of education about pregnancy).

But one thing should be emphasized in any setting: *The only sure way to prevent sexually transmitted diseases is to not engage in sexual behaviors.*

This is a hard, sad fact: Teens will be diagnosed with sexually transmitted diseases in large numbers. However, I've deliberately chosen not to emphasize STDs in this book for the following reasons:

- Diagnosing STDs should be left to medical professionals.
- Teens have gone tone-deaf about STDs: They tell me that adults emphasize STDs and pregnancy too much already in discussions about sexuality.
- Types of prevalent STDs change too rapidly for this book to be an accurate or complete resource.
- There is an abundance of available, up-to-date sources elsewhere to provide information on STDs.

Another factor you should always keep in mind when talking to your teens about sexual consequences is that the old "scared straight" method doesn't work. They can be completely grossed out when shown pictures of oozing STD lesions and yet their underdeveloped frontal-lobe thinking will assure them that this could never, ever happen to them.

Final Thoughts

While many behaviors that separate people from God don't visibly change a human body (you can watch porn and it not be obvious to someone when you're away from the computer, for instance), pregnancy and STDs can often be seen or perceived by others. In a way, they force the issue of teen sexuality when acted upon, demonstrate its cost when it's undeniable, and involve a whole family and a whole church.

And because God promises to work all circumstances together for good (even pregnancy and STDs), a parent with a teen in such difficult conditions can and should search for His promised redemptions of disasters. Furthermore, a parent in such a situation has a unique opportunity to do something extraordinary that gives us fellowship with God.

A parent can't step in to fix some situations no matter how earnestly we would like to repair them or rewind time. But like our Parent God who similarly does not fix most of the earthly results of our sins, we can and must be godlike in forgiveness. It's a loop: We forgive because we want and need forgiveness ourselves and won't get it if we refuse to forgive others (Mark 11:25; Matthew 6:14).

Your teen may be overwhelmed not only with earthly consequences but also with the thought that his or her sexual sin is so bad that God can't forgive it. A particularly helpful way of showing a teen that this isn't true is to take a globe of the world and put a finger on your geographical location. Then read Psalm 103:8–12:

> The LORD is compassionate and gracious,
>   slow to anger, abounding in love.
> He will not always accuse,
>   nor will he harbor his anger forever;
> he does not treat us as our sins deserve
>   or repay us according to our iniquities.
> For as high as the heavens are above the earth,
>   so great is his love for those who fear him;
> as far as the east is from the west,
>   so far has he removed our transgressions from us.

How far west can you go on the globe? Is there a point at which east meets west? No, the farther you go in one direction, you never meet up with the other direction—they are always separate. That's what God tells us about the place of our sins once He forgives them—we'll never meet them again.

EXPLORATION
WITH YOUR TEEN

1. Consider how many times in your life you've done something risky, thinking something like, "It's easier to get forgiveness than permission." Or how many times have you taken chances with behavior or relationships while depending on your own personal fable that says the bad results that happen to some people won't affect you? Does contemplating these things help you understand your teen better?

2. Read aloud and then discuss with your teen the following themes in Scripture:

   • God has a personal relationship with children in the uterus: Psalm 139:13–16; Jeremiah 1:5; Isaiah 44:24; Galatians 1:15.
   • Life is a gift only from God who creates it: Acts 17:25; 1 Timothy 6:13; Hebrews 9:27.
   • Taking a life from another innocent person is a sin: Deuteronomy 5:17.
   • How you regard life and death is a choice: Deuteronomy 30:19.
   • Children are to be seen as gifts from God: 1 Corinthians 6:19–20; Psalm 127:3.

3. Post the following verses where you and your teen can see them:

I, even I, am he who blots out
  your transgressions, for my own sake,
  and remembers your sins no more.

Isaiah 43:25

You will again have compassion on us; you will
tread our sins underfoot and hurl all our iniquities
into the depths of the sea.

Micah 7:19

If we claim to be without sin, we deceive ourselves
and the truth is not in us. If we confess our sins, he
is faithful and just and will forgive us our sins and
purify us from all unrighteousness.

1 John 1:8–9

FOURTEEN

The Balancing Act

Harnessing the Imagination of Your Teen

Jesus Christ is portrayed in the Bible with a multifaceted personality. Sure, He talked often of forgiving and love and friendship. But you can almost hear the chill in His voice when He said that anyone who hurt a kid should be thrown in the ocean with the first-century equivalent of cement overshoes (Matthew 18:6). He's taking names, and He's madder than blazes.

And we should take a step back in fear when we see the thundering hooves of a white horse bearing a Warrior with a sword coming out of His mouth, inviting birds to eat the flesh of His conquered enemies (Revelation 19:11–21).

And they are your enemies too.

Do your teens know about this? They are surrounded by CGI wonders. They are passively watching images that don't hold a candle to what can be produced by their imaginations interacting with true images you can introduce them to.

You may have to get wild and crazy here.

Sit down with your teen with no distractions and ask them to listen with their eyes closed to Zechariah chapters 1 through

6. (You may need to divide it into multiple sessions.) This is cool stuff! Angelic horses. Chariots. Stuffing an evil woman into a basket with a lead cover. Do you or your teen have to understand what it all means to get the big picture that God's not a wimp?

If your teen is discussing or reading online any of the godless arguments that advocate homosexual behavior, gender fluidity, body-modifying surgeries and hormones, abortion, or other current practices, the people who advocate these sins will tell your teen that the Bible doesn't address and certainly doesn't forbid some of these things. One of their favorite ploys is to say, "Look at all the laws in the Old Testament that seem to condemn homosexuality, for instance. But those same passages forbid eating shellfish, or they talk about stoning people and keeping slaves."

It's beyond the scope of this book but not beyond Google for you to find out, digest, and be able to help your teen understand the difference between (1) the ceremonial laws of the Old Testament, having to do with worship and keeping away from pagan practices; (2) the civil ones that were intended for the ancient city-state of Israel; and (3) the moral ones like the Ten Commandments, which are timeless in their concepts and call to holy behavior. No, we don't have to keep those ceremonial laws and civil ones either. But what were the principles behind them?

You may need to reciprocate when you ask your teen to mentally engage with Scripture: Show your willingness to see what they see in favorite musical artists, new artwork, runway models, even those who have made decisions to alter their bodies or adopt homosexual lifestyles. What makes these people tick? And without judgment, find out what makes these people attractive to your teen. You don't have to become hip, but you can be informed.

David's Story

When a young adult named David calls to make a counseling appointment, I am a little nervous. He'd spent countless hours over the span of a couple years meeting with me to help overcome what had become an entrenched pornography addiction he'd developed in his early teens. We had discussed masturbation, pornography, abortion, sexually transmitted diseases, and other topics. Much of our conversation focused on the negative consequences of sex rather than on the role of sex in marriage, but I kept reminding him that God created everyone as a sexual person, and that sex was a gift from Him for people, not a curse.

I hadn't heard from David for a couple of years, and I calculated that he must be halfway through college by now. He'd shown such dedication and progress that I suddenly fear he needs my help—has he fallen back into his old destructive habits?

To my delight, David enters the room and hand-delivers an invitation to his wedding with a lovely young woman named Becky. He also delivers some of the most affirming words anyone ever said to me.

"Dr. Beth, you helped me deal with some difficult stuff when I was in high school. You held my feet to the fire about the porn and got me to quit. I'm grateful for that, but I'm more grateful for all the conversations we had about God's plan for sex. Lots of my friends don't understand the role of sex in a marriage and that God intended for sex to create a special relationship between a husband and a wife."

"I'm glad all those discussions helped out." I, who have so many words, can't find many to express my feelings right now.

"The other thing, all those talks made it much easier for Becky and me to talk about sexual boundaries in our relationship and about sex once we are married. I don't think we could have waited for our wedding night if you hadn't talked with me so much. Thanks for taking time for me."

David's story drives home an important issue: Teens need someone to talk to. They crave something they can depend on, and staying the course of biblical teaching will be worth it, I assure you.

Overselling or Underselling Sex

Notice that this story gives some details about the reward of doing the right thing and postponing sex—of all varieties—until marriage. That is right and good.

But we can't make the mistake of lying to our children about the dual aspects of the nature of marriage. On the one hand, if "true love waits," as the messages of the past have told us, the act of obeying God's laws inherently brings rewards. We've learned that at the least, sex creates chemical reactions and bonds two people together in a way that nothing else in creation does.

But don't oversell this to your kids. Don't create another fantasy that will dishearten them eventually. What they experience will not *necessarily* be the mind-blowing sexual experiences that waiting sometimes brings. Intercourse between sexually inexperienced people can start out by being awkward and painful and confusing—and if they've been promised fireworks and chick-flick satisfaction, they are likely to be disappointed. It may take time and the essential trust that only a lifelong commitment produces to achieve true, lasting fulfillment. A recent study found that "when it comes to relationship quality in heterosexual relationships, highly religious couples enjoy higher-quality relationships and more sexual satisfaction, compared to less/mixed religious couples and secular couples."[1]

Gratification of all those saved-up treasures of intimacy is certainly good. But is that the end goal of a sexual relationship?

The other side of the coin in a Christian marriage is the aspect of self-sacrifice. Every parent knows that a marriage (of which sex is only a portion) can't exist long on passion. You can't build relationships on urges and needs. Successful marriages endure and prosper and bless man and wife, children and churches, and the whole world when they play out in real time the ethic of self-sacrifice. In Christian marriage, each partner cedes to the other dearly held preferences and privileges in order to serve unselfishly. They follow the example of Jesus, who gave up His right to rule the world when He came to serve it instead. It brought Him enormous pain temporarily, but eternal satisfaction.

Think about how His true love waited. He denied himself sexual satisfaction on earth (an honorable model for those who may never marry), but now pours out all His passion and love on a saved group of believers who, like Him, wait for something better than what this life has to offer. In the words of a friend of mine, One day, when our bodies and souls are reunited after death, this whole life thing "will be like a night in a bad hotel." Do you believe that? Do you as a parent know that? How can you phrase such things to your child so he or she will catch this vision?

You'll walk a tightrope here. You will have to express to your teen the enormous irony that although God created and heartily approves of sexual urges, He asks teens and adults not to act on those completely natural sexual urges except in marriage. Like morphine, whose effects it resembles, sex has a limited use and arena of operation. Shoot up all the time and you will end up with a wasted body and mind. Use it wisely and gratefully, and it blesses and comforts.

Sex isn't evil; it's enormously good. Like baptism, a marriage opens the door to a new life, with new responsibilities and new freedoms and new rewards that are worth waiting for on earth, with more to come later.

The earthly benefits aren't just theoretical. A recent CDC study shows that teens who practice sexual abstinence have other healthy behaviors too.[2] You're promoting their wholeness of health and stability when you model and reason with them about sexual self-control. But tell them another truth: Delaying acting upon, or refusing outright, sexual urges may be the anvil upon which celibate Christians are hammered out and refined, sometimes for years, sometimes for lifetimes. It is more and more common for Christians, especially women, to remain single by choice or by circumstance. Sometimes the ultimate reward is not seen here on earth.

Three Issues

As you begin to implement and strategize about how to engage the mind of your teen on sexual topics, there are two peripheral issues we should consider.

1. As you are open to talking to your teen about sexual issues, it may be that another teen will seek you out for advice. Remember that with our sexually charged social atmosphere and rampant accusations, you must be above reproach. You must balance two things: the openness of a teen to share their sexual struggles AGAINST the fact that you must *never ever* meet with a teen other than your own to discuss sexual issues alone or with a closed door. Seek out a public place where there will be no physical contact, where others can observe your actions. Do nothing other than listen dispassionately, and offer help if needed (for instance, if the teen is being abused or there is a legal issue of sex with someone older, or if the teen is pregnant). Do not promise confidentiality in such cases. You are bound by law and by morality to report such things

to the child's parents, and in cases of abuse, to legal authorities.

2. As you work through your own issues of sinfulness in the past, consider how much you need to share with your (spouse or) teen about your own possible past sexual sins. This is tricky, and you need to prepare for questions that will arise from your teen. Sometimes the solution is to delay giving specific information but to instead let them know that adults repent and sometimes pay for their sins for a long time.

James 1:5–7 has a remarkable promise that you should grab on to with both fists. Did you know there is a certain kind of prayer with a guaranteed good answer? It's the prayer for wisdom, which all parents need in abundance. "If any of you lacks wisdom, you should ask God, who gives generously to all without finding fault, and it will be given to you."

But there's a caution in the guarantee. "But when you ask, you must believe and not doubt, because the one who doubts is like a wave of the sea, blown and tossed by the wind. That person should not expect to receive anything from the Lord."

Trust God and ask for help with these issues.

Some Reminders

Relationship, relationship, relationship. All the Scriptures and strategies in the world you might know are unlikely to make an impact on your teen if you don't have the relationship to convey them and be heard. They will listen when they know you care, will respond when you listen without judgment and empathize with their struggles, will trust you when you can clarify issues with Scripture and role-play and suggest doable changes. *Who you are to them means more than anything you say.*

Prayer does change things. You have the ear of the Creator of the universe, and He inclines it to listen to your requests for your child. Don't give up, no matter what. Don't give up.

It all starts in the mind. Don't make the mistake of thinking that sexual sin is an outside enemy like pornography or social media or a seductive acquaintance who is storming the castle of your teen's sexuality. Remember Eve: The first sin of human history started when she used her mind to imagine what pleasant and intriguing results would come about if she did what she'd been told not to do. I think she must have been a teenager: She imagined before she tasted; she dismissed the possible consequences. James 1:14–15 paints the picture: "Each person is tempted when they are dragged away by their own evil desire and enticed. Then, after desire has conceived, it gives birth to sin; and sin, when it is full-grown, gives birth to death."

Keep reminding yourself that teens are unable to visualize bad consequences of their behavior because their frontal lobes are not developed enough. It's all about the personal fable we introduced in the chapter on physical and cognitive development. You're not going to scare them into avoiding bad consequences that they'll readily admit can happen to others, because they are utterly convinced those consequences won't happen to them personally. Unless such a thing has already touched their lives, they won't believe it. Woo their minds and souls with biblical truth about the rewards of operating on God's kindly intentioned agenda.

Speaking of fables, counter the world's idea that the Bible is only fable. You may not be able to convince the underdeveloped brain of your teen that they may suffer dreadful consequences from their sins, but you can counter other fables. Everything and everybody in the world will try to convince your teen that the Bible is only fable. Use resources to fight this tooth and nail. A very good book for this purpose is *Mama Bear Apologetics*.[3]

Think about the menu. From a teen's point of view, the future stretches out before them, full of choice and hope and freedom. In a way never before dreamed of, they can access innovative music, ideas, entertainment, and relationships. For the first time in history, the possibility of gender fluidity through sophisticated surgery and drug regimens is a reality. The natural teen inclination is to explore, to experiment, to sample the menu. There are so many wonders to experience in the exciting buffet line of life. Your job is to keep them from eating the puffer fish.

Think about the balancing act. For us, the issues are clear. We have the life experience to know that the kind of sexual freedom your teen is considering will lead to unwanted pregnancies, lifelong physical effects such as disease and addictions, unfixable broken relationships, enormous sadness and mourning, and perhaps the forfeiture of all God has planned for them in heaven. They see instead a different balancing act: a negotiation between their bodies and their minds, between you and them, between what the world says and what you say. In all of this, they are the centers of the universe and you must convince them that Someone else is just that.

Model godly access. There are so many characteristics of Jesus, God-in-flesh, that we want to both portray and stimulate in our children—focus, determination, courage, lovingkindness, creativity. We can also model another characteristic Jesus had: He didn't entrust himself to everyone. How do you replicate that while showing yourself to be kind toward others who are different? Your children will pick up on that. But you can teach this directly too, by sharing with them this startling insight: Jesus knew that people will let you down. In the case of people who'd seen His miracles and were all on board with Him, He still held himself in reserve:

> Now while he was in Jerusalem at the Passover Festival, many
> people saw the signs he was performing and believed in his

name. But *Jesus would not entrust himself to them, for he knew all people.* He did not need any testimony about mankind, for *he knew what was in each person.*

John 2:23–25 (italics added)

Express an eternal view, even if they can't "see" it. In your daily conversation, find ways to express to your children that for a Christian, life is a continuum that doesn't end at death. In fact, for a Christian, life never ends (John 11:25–26) but hurtles us body and soul toward a momentary separation of body and soul and then a spectacular reunion of the two in a limitless era of freedom from all troubles.

Your teen may have already watched a famous video of Francis Chan that you can easily find online.[4] In it, he uses a section of rope that's wrapped in red to demonstrate a lifetime. But then he pulls on the rope to reveal hundreds of additional feet of rope to illustrate the contrast between the length of any human life as compared with eternity. Assure your teen there is a calendar date coming when there won't be any questions about what's true and what's illusion. About who's right and who's wrong about sexual issues. Remind them of this verse in Psalm 73:20 about the enemies and troubles of this life: "They are like a dream when one awakes; when you arise, Lord, you will despise them as fantasies."

Everybody is tempted some way. Remind yourself that we can choose our careers, we can choose where we live, we can choose whom we marry, but we don't get to choose our temptations. Every sentient human in history with a beating heart and skin on them had temptations. They didn't choose what they were vulnerable to, and your teen and you don't get to choose either. Temptations are inevitable, and dealing with them is necessary for our growth and maturity. You don't pick *these* battles, just your responses to them.

Consider and honor the role of structure in life. The human desire for structure and order is as inherent as the order in DNA. It reflects a God who drove a wedge between light and dark and sealed that separation with His own oaths, who set limits on tsunamis, and who told people to put in place their own boundary stones, both real and figurative. He made some commandments so binary, so right-versus-wrong, that there's no second-guessing or negotiation: Don't murder, don't steal, honor your parents.

This same desire for order is deep inside your child, no matter how wild and free they desire to be. They crave the solidity of their parents and the anchor of a home, and find security in a reasoning approach when they have questions. Remember this is a temp job: You only have a few years with them in this peculiar relationship we call parenting. If you have to, put everything else on hold except life support and help your kids protect their sexual selves.

Final Thoughts

In a culture where we continually lower our expectations, don't give up your highest hopes for your children. You may be holding your breath, just trying to get your teen safely through to adulthood. But there's a much bigger picture. The world is holding its breath, waiting for the thought and morality and ethics leaders of tomorrow. Call your teen not just to sexual safety, but to nobility.

Tell them true stories about how they get to model extravagant eternal realities in front of a bankrupt world. About how self-sacrifice can be much more rewarding than self-gratification. Your son can be the Josiah, your daughter can be the Esther, who changes history because of the way they choose a higher path with their bodies and minds. And no matter how your lives will inevitably and rightly separate you from them, one day you'll get to have an eternity with them.

EXPLORING
WITH YOUR TEEN

1. There is abundant research that shows that the simple action of being thankful can reroute neural pathways in the brain and make your life more stable. With the conflicts that arise between teens and parents, you can keep yourself on point by buying a small paper journal in which you write daily at least one thing you like about your teen, or that you're grateful he or she has done that day. (Some days it may be something they didn't do.) Mention to them what you've noticed by saying something like "One thing I really appreciate about you is . . ."

2. Think of how this sequence works: Boundaries, accountability, repentance, restorative action. Think of a situation in which you are having to exercise personal self-control. How are you implementing this sequence in your own life? How can you share your struggles and successes with your teen?

3. If your spouse is not a Christian and your approach to teaching your teen sexual information differs from your spouse's, what strategies are you implementing? If you do have a Christian spouse and you disagree on how to talk to your teen about sexual matters, what resources are available to you? What if your spouse is either not a Christian or not in agreement with your approach to teens and sex?

4. How do you implement the wisdom of Jesus in His example in John 2:23–24? Which people and things do you not allow access to you?

5. Do you know godly parents who have successfully raised godly children? Instead of Googling every parenting problem, look to those people God has placed in your path. Ask them for counsel. And (gulp) ask them to critique your parenting. "Wounds from a friend can be trusted, but an enemy multiplies kisses" (Proverbs 27:6).

Recommended Resources

Books

Nancy Pearcey, *Love Thy Body: Answering Hard Questions about Life and Sexuality*. Ada, MI: Baker Books, 2018.

Hillary Morgan Ferrer, gen. ed., *Mama Bear Apologetics: Empowering Your Kids to Challenge Cultural Lies*. Eugene, OR: Harvest House, 2019.

Rosaria Champagne Butterfield, *Secret Thoughts of an Unlikely Convert: Expanded Edition*. Pittsburg: Crown & Covenant Publications; 2nd edition, 2014.

Lee Strobel and Jane Vogel, *The Case for Miracles Student Edition: A Journalist Explores the Evidence for the Supernatural*. Grand Rapids: Zondervan, Student Edition, 2018.

Michael S. Heiser, *The Unseen Realm: Recovering the Supernatural Worldview of the Bible*. Bellingham, WA: Lexham Press, 2019.

Beth Robinson, EdD, and Latayne Scott, PhD, *Protecting Your Child from Predators*. Bloomington, MN: Bethany House Publishers, 2019.

Jean E. Twenge, *iGen: Why Today's Super-Connected Kids Are Growing Up Less Rebellious, More Tolerant, Less Happy—and Completely Unprepared for Adulthood—and What That Means for the Rest of Us*. New York: Atria Paperback, 2018.

Shannon Ethridge and Stephen Arterburn, *Every Young Woman's Battle: Guarding Your Mind, Heart, and Body in a Sex-Saturated World (The Every Man Series)*. Colorado Springs: WaterBrook Press, 2009.

Stephen Arterburn, Fred Stoeker and Mike Yorkey, *Every Young Man's Battle: Strategies for Victory in the Real World of Sexual Temptation (The Every Man Series)*. Colorado Springs: WaterBrook Press, 2009.

Websites and Online Materials

Conversation Kits from Axis. https://axis.org/conversation-kits/

Center for Parent/Youth Understanding. https://cpyu.org/

Notes

Chapter 1: Get Real

1. Monica Anderson and Jingjing Jiang, "Teens, Social Media & Technology 2018," Pew Research Center, May 31, 2018, https://www.pewinternet.org/2018/05/31/teens-social-media-technology-2018.

2. Gigi Engle, "Anal Sex: Safety, How tos, Tips, and More: How to Do It the *Right* Way," *Teen Vogue*, November 12, 2019, https://www.teenvogue.com/story/anal-sex-what-you-need-to-know.

3. Center for Disease Control, National Center for HIV/AIDS, Viral Hepatitis, STD, and TB Prevention, 2015 National Youth Risk Behavior Survey, "Teen Pregnancy Prevention and United States Students," https://www.cdc.gov/healthyyouth/data/yrbs/pdf/2015/2015_us_pregnancy.pdf.

4. Jeremiah 9:24.

5. Genesis 5:2.

6. It is true that a minute percentage of people are born with indistinct genitalia. None of this is a modern issue: Jesus talks about people who are born as eunuchs—persons unable to reproduce—and elevates that as a calling to glorify God (Matthew 19:11–12). That, too, is a logo. Nothing ambushes God on such issues. He has thought this through already.

7. "I will not forget you! See, I have engraved you on the palms of my hands" (Isaiah 49:15–16).

Chapter 2: God's Plan for Sex

1. Jessica Roy, "Must Reads: How Millennials Replaced Religion with Astrology and Crystals," *Los Angeles Times*, July 10, 2019, https://www.latimes.com/health/la-he-millennials-religion-zodiac-tarot-crystals-astrology-20190710-story.html.

2. "For if the dead are not raised, then Christ has not been raised either. And if Christ has not been raised, your faith is futile; you are still in your sins. Then those also who have fallen asleep in Christ are lost. If only for this life we have hope in Christ, we

are of all people most to be pitied. But Christ has indeed been raised from the dead, the firstfruits of those who have fallen asleep" (1 Corinthians 15:16–20).

3. These are terrific: Conversation Kits from Axis, https://axis.org/conversation-kits/.

4. I believe the Bible teaches that we are actually triadic—body, spirit or thinking capacity, and soul or essence—but for purposes of discussion with teens, the idea of the physical and the spiritual is sufficient.

5. Not just in vitro fertilization and such anymore: Womb transplants are coming. Michael Cook, "Womb Transplants Could Be a 'Vital Medical Service' for Transgender Women," *BioEdge*, March 2, 2019, https://www.bioedge.org/bioethics/womb-transplants -could-be-a-vital-medical-service-for-transgender-women/12983.

6. There's one undeniable fact about a person's sex, according to cardiologist Paula Johnson: "Every cell has a sex . . . and what that means is that men and women are different down to the cellular and molecular levels. It means that we're different across all of our organs, from our brains to our hearts, our lungs, our joints." Paula Johnson, "His and Hers . . . Healthcare," TED Talk, January 22, 2014, https://www .youtube.com/watch?v=vhVWzkbAW4I.

7. Some popular teen resources skirt the issue by speaking of those who have prostates and those who have vaginas. Have pity on your poor kids, who are trying to navigate all this. We'll discuss later the facts about sex/gender being scientifically inarguable and unchangeable at the cellular level.

8. Genesis 2:24; Matthew 19:5–6; Mark 10:8; 1 Corinthians 6:16; Ephesians 5:31.

9. This is not just a lofty New Testament concept. The X-rated version of this is in Ezekiel chapter 16 and some say throughout the Song of Solomon as well.

10. Remember from chapter 1 that the Bible's use of the word *know* often implies a relationship as intimate as sex.

11. Micah 7:18–19 says,

Who is a God like you,
who pardons sin and forgives the transgression
of the remnant of his inheritance?
You do not stay angry forever
but delight to show mercy.
You will again have compassion on us;
you will tread our sins underfoot
and hurl all our iniquities into the depths of the sea.

12. John C. Maxwell, *Falling Forward: Turning Mistakes into Stepping Stones for Success* (Nashville, TN: Thomas Nelson, 2000), 114.

13. An excellent resource is Nancy Pearcey's *Love Thy Body: Answering Hard Questions about Life and Sexuality* (Baker Books, 2018).

Chapter 3: What's Happening Developmentally?

1. J. A. Graber, "Pubertal Timing and the Development of Psychopathology in Adolescence and Beyond," *Hormonal Behavior* 64, no. 2 (July 2013): 262–9.

2. K. Paige Harden and Elliot M. Tucker-Drob, "Individual Differences in the Development of Sensation Seeking and Impulsivity During Adolescence: Further Evidence for a Dual Systems Model," *Developmental Psychology*, 47, no. 3 (2011), 739–746.

3. Melanie J. Zimmer-Gembeck and Mark Helfand, "Ten Years of Longitudinal Research on U.S. Adolescent Sexual Behavior: Developmental Correlates of Sexual

Intercourse, and the Importance of Age, Gender and Ethnic Background," *Developmental Review* 28, no. 2 (2008), 153–224, https://doi.org/10.1016/j.dr.2007.06.001.

4. Simmons and Blyth, *Moving into Adolescence.*

5. American Academy of Pediatrics, "American Academy of Pediatrics Study Documents Early Puberty Onset in Boys," October 20, 2012, https://www.eurekalert.org/pub_releases/2012-10/aaop-aao_2101312.php.

6. Dominic Hernandez, "The Decreasing Age of Puberty," *Vital Record: News from Texas A & M Health Sciences Center*, January 16, 2018, https://vitalrecord.tamhsc.edu/decreasing-age-puberty/.

7. Luke 2:41–52.

8. Barton D. Schmitt, "Masturbation in Preschoolers," Summit Medical Group Foundation, 2014, https://www.summitmedicalgroup.com/library/pediatric_health/pa-hhgbeh_masturbation/.

9. Cynthia L. Robbins, Vanessa Schick, Michael Reece, et al., "Prevalence, Frequency, and Associations of Masturbation with Partnered Sexual Behaviors Among US Adolescents," *Archives of Pediatric Adolescent Medicine* 165, no. 12 (2011):1087–1093.

10. In Old Testament times, a childless widow had no social security to depend on, and God instituted levirate marriage, the practice of the brother of a deceased man taking into his household his brother's widow and carrying on that man's family line by impregnating her with children who would bear the deceased man's name.

11. Patrick L. Hill, Peter M. Duggan, and Daniel K. Lapsley, "Subjective Invulnerability, Risk Behavior, and Adjustment in Early Adolescence," The Journal of Early Adolescence 32, no. 4 (2012): 489–501; and Holly E. R. Morrell, Daniel K. Lapsley, and Bonnie L. Halpern-Felsher, "Subjective Invulnerability and Perceptions of Tobacco-Related Benefits Predict Adolescent Smoking Behavior," *The Journal of Early Adolescence* (2015), DOI:10.1177/0272431615578274.

Chapter 4: How Teens Relate to Others

1. Jack Martin and Bryan Sokol, "Generalized Others and Imaginary Audience: A Neo-Meadian Approach to Adolescent Egocentrism," *New Ideas in Psychology* 29, no. 3 (2011): 364–375.

2. Graham Jackson, "The Empty Chair," *International Journal of Clinical Practice* 60, no. 12 (2006): 1519.

3. A non-Christian physician who writes under the name of Theodore Dalrymple asserts that only by resisting bad impulses can one overcome them. His work with heroin addicts led him to conclude that any bad impulse only gets worse if you give in to it. See *Spoilt Rotten: The Toxic Cult of Sentimentality* (Gibson Square Books, 2011) and other of his books to see this.

4. First Corinthians 10:13 (HCSB) is a good verse to memorize with your teen: "No temptation has overtaken you except what is common to humanity. God is faithful, and He will not allow you to be tempted beyond what you are able, but with the temptation He will also provide a way of escape so that you are able to bear it."

5. It's true that this statement occurs in the midst of Paul's discussion of the chaos of many people all trying to communicate in a way unintelligible to others. But does that not describe teens and parents?

6. Jeremiah 1:4–8 and 29:11–13.

7. 2 Corinthians 12:7–10.

Chapter 5: You Want Me to Talk about S-E-X?

1. Robert Weiss, "Prevalence of Porn," *Sex and Intimacy in a Digital Age* (blog), *Psych Central*, March 28, 2019, https://blogs.psychcentral.com/sex/2013/05/the-prevalence -of-porn/.

2. Personal correspondence from John Delony to Beth Robinson.

3. Remember this terrific visual image shared in footnote 12 of chapter 2, from Micah 7:18–19: "Who is a God like you, who pardons sin and forgives the transgression of the remnant of his inheritance? You do not stay angry forever but delight to show mercy. You will again have compassion on us; you will tread our sins underfoot and hurl all our iniquities into the depths of the sea."

Chapter 6: Intimacy and Boundaries

1. Tim Challies, "The Joys (and the Limitations) of Male-Female Friendships," @ *Challies* (blog), September 19, 2018, https://www.challies.com/articles/thinking-through -male-female-friendships/.

2. Job 38:8–11 and Proverbs 8:29.

3. Numbers 35:22–25.

4. Jeffrey M. Henderson, "Teaching Abstinence" brochure (University of Texas–Houston Medical School, 2001), 6.

5. Many Christians have noted that public sex education seems as much recruitment for ungodly sexual practices as it is about sex. This intensifies when teens encounter "sex week" on college campuses that provide even more explicit how-to instructions for sex outside of marriage and outside of God's approval.

6. Henderson, "Teaching Abstinence."

7. Theresa Crenshaw in Jennifer Roback Morse, *The Sexual Revolution and Its Victims* (Ruth Institute Books, 2015), 138.

8. "Spiked: Exploring Substance Spiking in America," Alcohol.org, https://www.alcohol .org/guides/spiked/. See also Linda Carroll, "Drink Spiking at College May Be More Common Than Thought," *NBC News*, May 28, 2016, https://www.nbcnews.com/feat ure/college-game-plan/drink-spiking-college-may-be-more-common-thought-n581881.

Chapter 7: Understanding Relationships

1. Amanda Lenhart, Monica Anderson, Aaron Smith, "Teens, Technology and Romantic Relationships: Introduction," Pew Research Center, October 1, 2015, https:// www.pewinternet.org/2015/10/01/teens-technology-and-romantic-relationships/.

2. Lenhart, Anderson, and Smith, "Teens, Technology."

3. Lenhart, Anderson, and Smith, "Teens, Technology."

4. Lenhart, Anderson, and Smith, "Teens, Technology."

5. Lenhart, Anderson, and Smith, "Teens, Technology."

6. Lenhart, Anderson, and Smith, "Teens, Technology."

7. Centers for Disease Control and Prevention, "Over Half of U.S. Teens Have Had Sexual Intercourse by Age 18, New Report Shows," June 22, 2017, https://www.cdc .gov/nchs/pressroom/nchs_press_releases/2017/201706_NSFG.htm.

8. Nancy Pearcey, *Love Thy Body: Answering Hard Questions about Life and Sexuality* (Ada, MI: Baker Books, 2018), 149.

9. Romans 12:10.

10. Gabby, "Teaching Teen Dating Skills," *The Dating Divas* (blog), December 17, 2015, https://www.thedatingdivas.com/teaching-teen-dating-skills.

11. United States Census Bureau (October 10, 2019), Historical Marital Status Tables, https://www.census.gov/data/tables/time-series/demo/families/marital.html.

12. Jeremiah 16:1–4; 1 Corinthians 7:8—which, while advocating the unmarried status, continues on in later verses to discuss that if sexual passion is too great, it's better to marry.

13. Pearcey, *Love Thy Body*, 144. Italics in original.

Chapter 8: Sexual Abuse and Violence

1. "Should not shepherds take care of the flock? You eat the curds, clothe yourselves with the wool and slaughter the choice animals, but you do not take care of the flock. You have not strengthened the weak or healed the sick or bound up the injured. You have not brought back the strays or searched for the lost."

2. U.S. Department of Justice, Office of Justice Programs, Bureau of Justice Statistics, "Sexual Assault of Young Children as Reported to Law Enforcement" (2000).

3. Laura Hawks, et al., "Association Between Forced Sexual Initiation and Health Outcomes Among US Women," *JAMA Internal Medicine*, 179, no. 11 (September 16, 2019): 1551–1558, doi:10.1001/jamainternmed/2019/3500.

Chapter 9: Social Media and Technology

1. "Teenage Sexting Statistics," GuardChild.com, accessed December 1, 2019, http://www.guardchild.com/teenage-sexting-statistics/.

2. "Teenage Sexting," GuardChild.com.

3. "Teenage Sexting," GuardChild.com.

4. "Teenage Sexting," GuardChild.com.

5. "Teenage Sexting," GuardChild.com.

6. "Teenage Sexting," GuardChild.com.

7. "Internet Statistics," GuardChild.com, accessed December 1, 2019, https://www.guardchild.com/statistics/.

8. "Internet Statistics," GuardChild.com.

9. "Teenage Sexting Statistics," GuardChild.com.

10. "Internet Statistics," GuardChild.com.

11. "Social Media Statistics," GuardChild.com, accessed December 1, 2019, https://www.guardchild.com/social-media-statistics-2/.

12. "Social Media," GuardChild.com.

13. "Social Media," GuardChild.com.

14. "Social Media," GuardChild.com.

15. "Social Media," GuardChild.com.

Chapter 10: This Is Your Teen's Brain on Porn

1. Tim Challies, "Children and Pornography—Three-Minute Thursdays #2," @ *Challies* (blog), November 9, 2017, https://www.challies.com/vlog/children-and-pornography-three-minute-thursdays-2/.

2. "Internet Statistics," GuardChild.com, accessed December 1, 2019, https://www.guardchild.com/statistics/.

3. "Internet Statistics," GuardChild.com.

4. "Internet Statistics," GuardChild.com.

5. "Internet Statistics," GuardChild.com.

6. Covenant Eyes, *Porn Stats, 250+ Facts, Quotes, and Statistics about Pornography Use* (2018 edition), https://www.covenanteyes.com/resources/download-your-copy -of-the-pornography-statistics-pack/, page 15.

7. "Report Shows 60% of Students Turn to Porn to Learn about Sex," *Fight the New Drug*, August 6, 2019, https://fightthenewdrug.org/see-how-many-students-use -porn-to-learn-about-sex/.

8. Imogen Parker, *Young People, Sex and Relationships: The New Norms* (London: Institute for Public Policy Research, 2014), 24, https://www.ippr.org/files/publication s/pdf/young-people-sex-relationships_Aug2014.pdf.

9. Simone Kühn and Jürgen Gallinat, "Brain Structure and Functional Connectiv-ity Associated with Pornography Consumption: The Brain on Porn," *Journal of the American Medical Association Psychiatry* 71, no. 7 (July 2014): 827–834.

10. Jennifer Riemersma and Michael Sytsma, "A New Generation of Sexual Ad-diction," *Sexual Addiction & Compulsivity* 20, no. 4 (October 2013): 306–322, http:// www.ingentaconnect.com/content/routledg/usac/2013/00000020/00000004/art0000 6?crawler=true.

11. Kühn and Gallinat, "Brain Structure and Functional Connectivity."

12. Valerie Voon, et al., "Neural Correlates of Sexual Cue Reactivity in Individuals with and without Compulsive Sexual Behaviours," University of Cambridge, 2014, ac-cessed December 29, 2015, http://journals.plos.org/plosone/article?id=10.1371/journal .pone.0102419.

13. Nancy Pearcey, *Love Thy Body: Answering Hard Questions about Life and Sexuality* (Ada, MI: Baker Books, 2018), 128.

14. Dr. Janet Zadina, personal correspondence with Dr. Scott, September 23, 2019.

15. Susan Villani, "Impact of Media on Children and Adolescents: A 10-Year Review of the Research," *Journal of the American Academy of Child & Adolescent Psychiatry* 40, no. 4 (April 2001): 392, 399.

16. Jochen Peter and Patti Valkenburg, "Adolescents and Pornography: A Review of 20 Years of Research," *Journal of Sex Research* 53, no. 4–5 (2016): 509–531.

17. Riemersma and Sytsma, "New Generation of Sexual Addiction."

18. Riemersma and Sytsma, "New Generation of Sexual Addiction."

19. Wording from the NIV in Jeremiah 7:31, 19:5, 32:35.

20. Chiara Sabina, Janis Wolak, and David Finkelhor, "The Nature and Dynamics of Internet Pornography Exposure for Youth," *CyberPsychology and Behavior* 11, no. 6 (2008): 691–693.

21. Sabina, Wolak, and Finkelhor, "Internet Pornography Exposure."

22. Sabina, Wolak, and Finkelhor, "Internet Pornography Exposure."

23. Imogen Parker, *Young People, Sex, and Relationships*, 22.

24. Melinda Selmys, *Sexual Authenticity: An Intimate Reflection on Homosexuality and Catholicism* (Huntington, IN: Our Sunday Visitor, 2009), 83.

25. Billy Graham, *The Holy Spirit: Activating God's Power in Your Life* (Reissue edition) (Nashville: Thomas Nelson, 2011), 94.

Chapter 11: Disorienting Sexuality

1. Centers for Disease Control and Prevention, *Sexual Identity, Sex of Sexual Contacts, and Health-Risk Behaviors Among Students in Grades 9–12: United States*

and Selected Sites, 2015 (Atlanta, GA: U.S. Department of Health and Human Services, 2016), https://www.cdc.gov/mmwr/volumes/65/ss/pdfs/ss6509.pdf.

2. Centers for Disease Control and Prevention, *Sexual Identity*, 2016.

3. Centers for Disease Control, *Sexual Identity*, 2016.

4. Christopher Yuan and Angela Yuan, *Out of a Far Country: A Gay Son's Journey to God. A Broken Mother's Search for Hope* (Colorado Springs, CO: WaterBrook, 2011), 187.

Chapter 12: Understanding Gender Issues

1. Michelle M. Johns et al., "Transgender Identity and Experiences of Violence Victimization, Substance Use, Suicide Risk, and Sexual Risk Behaviors Among High School Students—19 States and Large Urban School Districts, 2017," *Morbidity and Mortality Weekly Report* 68, no. 3 (January 25, 2019): 67–71, DOI: http://dx.doi.org /10.15585/mmwr.mm6803a3.

2. Sari L. Reisner et al., "Gender Minority Social Stress in Adolescence: Disparities in Adolescent Bullying and Substance Use by Gender Identity," *Journal of Sex Research*, 52, no. 3 (2015): 243–56, published online April 17, 2014.

3. Reisner et al., "Gender Minority Social Stress."

4. Johns et al., "Transgender Identity."

5. Barna Group and Impact 360 Institute, *Gen Z: The Culture, Beliefs and Motivations Shaping the Next Generation* (2018), 46–47.

6. Kate Shellnutt, "Get Ready, Youth Group Leaders: Teens Twice as Likely to Identify as Atheist or LGBT," *Christianity Today*, January 23, 2018, https://www .christianitytoday.com/news/2018/january/youth-group-leaders-generation-z-atheis -lgbt-teens-barna.html.

7. Steven Collins and Latayne C. Scott, *Discovering the City of Sodom: The Fascinating, True Account of the Discovery of the Old Testament's Most Infamous City* (New York: Howard Books, 2016).

8. Acts 17:27.

9. Ecclesiastes 3:11.

10. This may not be a good discussion topic for your child, but you might consider that God has no genitalia nor bodily DNA and thus is not of any sex. True, He specifically and deliberately chose to be addressed as *He*, and His relationship to people as Bridegroom to Bride. Whatever it means for earthly relationships, He, with very few exceptions, portrays himself as King, Warrior, Protector, Leader, Defender, and other roles.

11. Michael W. Chapman, "John Hopkins Psychiatrist: Transgender is 'Mental Disorder;' Sex Change 'Biologically Impossible,'" *CNS News*, June 2, 2015, https:// www.cnsnews.com/news/article/michael-w-chapman/johns-hopkins-psychiatrist -transgender-mental-disorder-sex-change, which is based on the *Wall Street Journal* article it references.

12. More and more young people are uncomfortable dealing with transgenderism and other forms of sexual variation. *New York* magazine columnist and avowed homosexual Andrew Sullivan quotes statistics from gender-inclusive organization GLAAD that show there is a significantly decreasing percentage of Americans who are comfortable with LGBTQ people. While older people may have a stable level of tolerance, in the age group eighteen to thirty-four, 63 percent were comfortable in 2016 whereas

only 45 percent were in 2018, according to "The Gender-Theory Backlash" online at http://nymag.com/intelligencer/2019/06/andrew-sullivan-democrats-are-in-a-bubble -on-immigration.html. Sullivan attributes this to the fact that the gay-left culture has morphed into a "trans movement."

13. Feminists used to be the great allies of the transsexual community too, but many are seeing the logical outcome of letting bigger, stronger, biologically male contestants compete with women. This affects everything from athletic records to scholarships.

14. Karen L. Blair and Rhea Ashley Hoskin, "Transgender Exclusion from the World of Dating: Patterns of Acceptance and Rejection of Hypothetical Trans Dating Partners as a Function of Sexual and Gender Identity," *Journal of Social and Personal Relationships*, May 31, 2018, https://journals.sagepub.com/doi/abs/10.1177/0265407518779139.

15. Rosaria Butterfield, "Love Your Neighbor Enough to Speak Truth: A Response to Jen Hatmaker," *The Gospel Coalition*, October 31, 2016, https://www.thegospel coalition.org/article/love-your-neighbor-enough-to-speak-truth/.

16. Jonathon Van Maren, "Prominent Gay Atheist: Transgenderism Is a 'Lie.' Agreeing to It Demoralizes You," LifeSiteNews.com, May 30, 2019, https://www.lifesitenews .com/blogs/prominent-gay-atheist-transgenderism-is-a-lie.

Chapter 13: Unplanned and Unexpected

1. Lisa Romero et al., "Reduced Disparities in Birth Rates Among Teens Aged 15–19 Years—United States, 2006–2007 and 2013–2014," *Morbidity and Mortality Weekly Report* 65, no. 16 (2016): 409–414.

2. Patricia E. Donaldson, MSW; Margaret H. Whalen; and Jeane W. Anastas, PhD; "Teen Pregnancy and Sexual Abuse: Exploring the Connection," *Smith College Studies in Social Work* 59, no. 3 (1989): 289–300.

3. Kathryn Kost and Isaac Maddow-Zimet, *U.S. Teenage Pregnancies, Births and Abortions, 2011: State Trends by Age, Race and Ethnicity* (New York: Guttmacher Institute, 2016), https://www.guttmacher.org/report/us-teen-pregnancy-state-trends-2011.

4. Gladys M. Martinez and Joyce C. Abma, "Sexual Activity, Contraceptive Use, and Childbearing of Teenagers Aged 15–19 in the United States," National Center for Health Statistics Data Brief, no. 209 (July 2015), https://www.cdc.gov/nchs/data /databriefs/db209.pdf.

5. Martinez, and Abma, "Sexual Activity."

6. The Bible does not mention, nor directly address, the practice of abortion. However, some people believe that Exodus 21:22–25 sheds some light on the issue. In it, legal penalties are outlined for injury in the case of a pregnant woman who becomes involved in a physical fight between two men. The passage is hard to understand but many interpret it to say that the premature birth of her child (and the child's possible death) carries a lesser penalty than if she herself is injured. The implication, they would say, is that the life of a fetus is not legally equal to that of its mother. But even abortion advocates will admit that this scenario is an accidental situation, not a planned abortion.

7. It's not a solution, and abortion is not a modern invention. People have used drugs and devices for thousands of years to cause the death of unborn children and throughout all the writings of the early church onward, abortion was always condemned as the unjustifiable taking of a human life. Only in very recent years have churches advocated it, and they are typically churches that also condone other ungodly practices.

8. Among those who are pro-abortion and those who are opposed to it, there is no consensus on the issue of exactly at which point of development—conception? first heartbeat? viability? exit from the mother's body? ability to reason and communicate?—someone becomes fully human.

9. From Dr. Scott: Another startling fact reminds us of the consequences of killing a child. This one blows me away. Every baby girl is born with every egg she will ever have in her ovaries. They will mature on schedule throughout her childbearing years, but they are all within her before she is born. If you combine that with God's understanding that some aspect of all males is somehow similarly present in the bodies of their ancestors (Hebrews 7:10), that means an abortion isn't just the taking of a single life, but in essence the taking of unnumbered additional ones who will never see the light of birth.

10. Centers for Disease Control and Prevention, "New CDC Report: STDs Continue to Rise in the U.S.," October 8, 2019, https://www.cdc.gov/nchhstp/newsroom /2019/2018-STD-surveillance-report-press-release.html?deliveryName=USCDC-24 3-DM10502.

11. Centers for Disease Control and Prevention, "Sexually Transmitted Diseases: Adolescents and Young Adults," n.d., page last reviewed December 7, 2017, https:// www.cdc.gov/std/life-stages-populations/adolescents-youngadults.htm.

Chapter 14: The Balancing Act

1. Institute for Family Studies, "The Ties that Bind: Is Faith a Global Force for Good or Ill in the Family?" *World Family Map 2019*, https://ifstudies.org/reports/world -family-map/2019/executive-summary.

2. Centers for Disease Control and Prevention, "Youth Risk Behavior Surveillance — United States, 2017," June 15, 2018, https://www.cdc.gov/mmwr/volumes/67/ss/ss 6708a1.htm?s_cid=ss6708a1_; Roberta G. Simmons and Dale A. Blyth, *Moving into Adolescence: The Impact of Pubertal Change and School Context* (Hawthorn, NY: Aldine, de Gruyter, 1987). Melanie J. Zimmer-Gembeck and Mark Helfand, "Ten Years of Longitudinal Research on U.S. Adolescent Sexual Behavior: Developmental Correlates of Sexual Intercourse and the Importance of Age, Gender and Ethnic Background, *Developmental Review* 28, no. 2 (June 2008):153–224.

3. Hillary Morgan Ferrer, gen. ed., *Mama Bear Apologetics: Empowering Your Kids to Challenge Cultural Lies* (Eugene, OR: Harvest House, 2019).

4. Francis Chan, *Francis Chan - Rope Illustration (Original)*, YouTube.com, April 1, 2010, https://www.youtube.com/watch?v=86dsfBbZfWs.

Beth Robinson, EdD, is a professor of psychology at Lubbock Christian University, a visiting lecturer in the Clinical Mental Health Counseling program at Harding University, and was previously a professor of pediatrics at Texas Tech University Health Sciences Center. She is a licensed professional counselor, an approved supervisor for licensed professional counselors, and a certified school counselor. She has used those credentials to work with abused and traumatized children for more than twenty-five years as a counselor. Beth has also lived with foster and adoptive children in her home and has written books for professionals, parents, and children.

Latayne C. Scott, PhD, is the author of more than two dozen books, both fiction and nonfiction, and hundreds of published shorter works. She is Trinity Southwest University's Author in Residence and is the recipient of Pepperdine University's Distinguished Christian Service Award and numerous other awards for her writing.

More from Beth Robinson and Latayne C. Scott

Research shows that one in four females and one in six males are sexually abused before age 18—and the enemy is commonly someone you know and trust. Providing expert advice, Dr. Beth Robinson offers effective steps to help you ensure you're reducing the risks of abuse. Move from fear to confidence on this heavy topic that's too important to ignore!

Protecting Your Child from Predators

◊ BETHANYHOUSE

Stay up to date on your favorite books and authors with our free e-newsletters. Sign up today at bethanyhouse.com.

 facebook.com/BHPnonfiction

 @bethany_house

 @bethany_house_nonfiction